THE WISDOM OF WALT

LEADERSHIP LESSONS FROM THE HAPPIEST PLACE ON EARTH

JEFFREY A. BARNES

The Wisdom of Walt: Leadership Lessons from the Happiest Place on Earth

Published by:
Aviva Publishing
Lake Placid, NY
518-523-1320
www.AvivaPubs.com

Jeff Barnes
Email: jeff@thewisdomofwalt.com
www.thewisdomofwalt.com

The Wisdom of Walt and Aviva Publishing are not associated with The Walt Disney Company.

ISBN: 978-1-947937-24-6

Library of Congress Control Number: 2015907704

Editor: Tyler Tichelaar, Superior Book Productions
Cover Designers: Kyle Ready and Nicole Gabriel
Interior Book Layout: Choi Messer

Every attempt has been made to source properly all quotes.
Printed in the United States of America
New Edition

2 4 6 8 10 12

This book is dedicated to my wife, Niki.
Every day, you prove that Disneyland doesn't lie; dreams really do come true. Thanks for being my wish. My star. My princess.

"Disneyland liberates men to their better selves. Here the wild brute is gently corralled, not used and squashed, not put upon and harassed, not trapped on by real-estate operators, nor exhausted by smog and traffic."

— Ray Bradbury, author

"I hold a view that may be somewhat shocking to an audience as sophisticated as this, and this is, that the greatest piece of design in the United States today is Disneyland. If you think about Disneyland and think of its performance in relationship to its purpose—its meaning to people more than its meaning to the process of development—you will find it the outstanding piece of urban design in the United States. It took an area of activity—the amusement park—and lifted it to a standard so high in its performance, in its respect for people, in its functioning for people, that it really became a brand new thing. It fulfills the functions that it set out to accomplish unself-consciously, usefully and profitably. I find more to learn in the standards that have been set and the goals that have been achieved in the development of Disneyland than in any other single piece of physical development in the country."

— James Rouse, noted designer, in a commencement speech at the Harvard School of Design in 1963

CONTENTS

A NOTE TO THE READER

THIS IS NOT AN ACADEMIC work but one for the general reader. Just as Walt Disney wouldn't have wanted to destroy the magic of watching *Snow White and the Seven Dwarfs* by stopping the film to explain his research into fairy tales and why he depicted the characters as he did or to present the details of how many drawings are needed to create a full-length animated film, I didn't want to cause readers to be interrupted in the reading process by needless footnotes. However, all the information contained in this book may be relied upon as accurate and derived from the sources found in the bibliography at the end.

FOREWORD
BY GARNER HOLT & BILL BUTLER

World's Largest Maker of Audio-Animatronics

THIS BOOK IS A CHRONICLE of one of the biggest and most unlikely success stories in the business or entertainment worlds. At least, we see the early chapters of the Disneyland story that way today.

The Disneyland dream was almost over before it had even begun. Walt Disney struggled for years to find the financial and political support to make his vision of a new kind of experiential family entertainment a reality. Like many dreamers, Walt could see what other people couldn't. He understood the post-war American public's pining for an innovative, clean, user-friendly attraction. Disneyland was not to be merely a creative expression built for its own benefit: it had to be a profitable business and diversification of Disney's already powerful global media corporation. (We understand a little bit of that here at Garner Holt Productions, Inc.—magic is a difficult business machine to feed!)

Renowned for his business and creative prowess at the helm of a significant film studio with valuable merchandising and publishing interests, Walt faced enormous adversity in introducing the Disneyland entertainment concept to the world—simply put, to most investors, the park appeared to be a losing venture, too bold, too new, too incredible to attach to a realistic business model. "I could never convince the financiers that Disneyland was feasible," Walt said. "Because dreams offer too little collateral." Bill's grandfather was president of a local bank in the early 1950s and recalls meeting with representatives from Disney, who were trying to obtain financial backing for the park. He (and many others like him) passed on the opportunity, to his lifelong regret.

Disneyland's biggest champion (and also one of the world's greatest communicators) could do little to prove his dreams were viable other than to build them, to translate from paper and paint to steel and concrete. Walt was an action leader, a dynamic mover, always pressing for more, bigger, better, newer. Disneyland was the ultimate expression of leading through action in Walt's time—and in any time since, really. It created a whole new market, changed travel dynamics worldwide, and planted the seeds of new cultures for both designers and consumers.

Of course, not all dreams turn out the way Disneyland did. Sometimes, the right alignment of talents, time, ideas, and money never comes. It's the special dreamer (and leader) who keeps the flame of interest, of promise and hope, lit to guide not merely himself, but those who would be an audience to the dream. The stories told by Dr. Barnes in this book—of Walt, Disneyland, and his own personal stories—illustrate the fundamental truths of all dreamer-leaders, for all leaders must have vision for themselves to make it apparent to others.

We understand that intimately at Garner Holt Productions. Garner's story is all about that: a teenager with a vision for creating a viable, profitable company to produce animatronics. Like Walt, Garner's fantastic, magical product wasn't the most apparent business model. Only through tenacity, through *showing* people what the business would do, and by playing the role of dreamer-leader could Garner turn a personal passion into a respected company—in fact, the largest animatronics company in the world. Much of that was because Walt is such an influence on our company. In fact, even today, with every project we complete for Disney theme parks around the world, we say, "We're working for Walt." It's his passion for innovation, quality, and imagination that inspires us to give our clients more than what they ask for.

Dr. Barnes has added to the Disneyland canon a unique take on the park that we very dearly love. For his narrative, Disneyland is not merely the greatest themed experience in the world; it is the direct product of innovative and careful leadership. He captures the intricacies of theme park design (they are often annoyingly intricate…) from Walt's time to now, painting a living portrait of the park as a series of deliberate decisions, inspirations, failures, and triumphs. This is Disneyland as few have considered it, sixty years after proving Walt was the greatest dreamer-leader the world has ever known.

As a business, our company learns from many sources all the time. There's always a new method or material, a new component or approach for our work in designing themed attractions and creating amazing animatronics. But we always turn to Walt's park for the biggest lessons. Disneyland is still the ultimate expression of the creative arts: it *is* film, it *is* theater, it *is* fine art, it *is* architecture, it *is* history, it *is* music. Disneyland offers to us professionally (and to everyone who seeks it) a primer in bold imagination in nearly every genre imaginable.

And most of all, Disneyland is a temple to Walt's unique brand of leadership. What follows in these pages is a prism for you to see the park the way we do, too. Don't forget to get your Disneyland handstamp at the end. We're sure you'll want to return to this magical story many times.

INTRODUCTION

TO ALL WHO READ THIS HAPPY BOOK

EACH TIME YOU ENTER DISNEYLAND, a cast member offers you a Guidemap. This gives you a lay of the land and allows you to plan your day around the various attractions, restaurants, stores, shows, parades, and fireworks.

Before you enter the world I have created in this book, I, too, want to provide you with a "map." This orientation will guide and assist you in getting value from this book long after you finish reading.

First, below each chapter title is a quote from Walt Disney. This quote represents the kernel of Walt's wisdom that we will explore in that chapter's pages. Second, just as a day at Disneyland begins and ends on Main Street, U.S.A., each chapter begins and ends with a story about Disneyland. Walt once said, "Disneyland is the star. Everything else is the supporting role." Disneyland is the "star" of this book. "The Happiest Place on Earth" has the lead role in teaching us valuable lessons about life, leadership, success, and happiness.

As you will learn, Walt created Disneyland as a visual showpiece for storytelling. After controlling the "opening shot" on Main Street, Walt wanted his guests to choose their own stories and adventures via the various attractions located throughout the park. It is fitting, then, that I share with you some of my own stories and adventures. The tales are true and represent themes we all have in common: work, family, childhood, success, failure, and love. This isn't a love story per se; however, you need to know I am madly in love with my wife, Niki, and our story drives more than a few of the stories in this book.

Each morning, during the exciting ritual of "rope drop" on Main Street, the announcer declares Disneyland as the place where "dreams really do come true." Today, I am living my dream by teaching a college-level course at California Baptist University in Riverside, California: The History of Disneyland. Yes, you can get college credit for this class; it counts toward the General Education requirement of U.S. History. Space is limited, however, so this book is my attempt to deliver critical course content to a larger audience. How this class came to be, the challenges I faced along the way, and the educational experience that ensued are also part of the journey ahead.

Finally, each chapter contains a "Souvenir Stop." Here you will find the "take-home exercises" for that chapter's lesson. Souvenirs serve as keepsakes and mementos of places we have been and events we want to remember. I hope you'll want to take the lessons you learn in *The Wisdom of Walt: Leadership Lessons from the Happiest Place on Earth* "home" with you.

Please don't set your souvenirs on a shelf or allow them to disappear in a forgotten drawer. I believe it is possible to live every day as if it's a day at Disneyland. It isn't always easy; too often the real world is filled with more problems than pixie dust.

My advice?

Listen to the park.

Walt envisioned Disneyland to be "...a live, breathing thing." Like any person, the park has its own personality. It has stood the test of time; its history and stories speak to anyone who will listen. Open your heart and you might discover the Wisdom of Walt and his Magic Kingdom.

Mickey Mouse Ears not required.

SITTING ON A PARK BENCH

"If you can dream it, you can do it."

YOUR FAVORITE ATTRACTION

WHAT IS YOUR FAVORITE DISNEYLAND attraction? We all have one. If you don't, then I doubt you would bother reading this book.

Is yours Space Mountain?

Perhaps Pirates of the Caribbean? Maybe the Matterhorn Bobsleds?

Or do you prefer the Indiana Jones Adventure?

For some, the favorite is "it's a small world". Others, like my wife, have a preference for Peter Pan's Flight.

Regardless of your personal favorite, your favorite is just that, personal.

Mine is a bit more pedestrian. In fact, my favorite attraction really isn't an attraction at all. At least not in the traditional sense. It isn't a ride that will spin you, a coaster that will drop you, or even a show that will mesmerize you. You can't find it on a park map, nor can you read about it in a guidebook. It is there, nonetheless, and it exists only in Disneyland. It has not, nor can it ever be, replicated in any other Disney park anywhere else in the world.

My favorite attraction is a mere park bench.

Disneyland is filled with park benches. This is no accident. Walt Disney intentionally built Disneyland to be a park, a place where people could sit, enjoy the themed environments, and be enveloped by memories of an earlier and easier time. At Disneyland, Disneyland itself is the main attraction. The rides and shows take second billing.

My favorite attraction is a park bench. But it is the only bench in the entire park that you cannot actually sit on. It is the oldest bench in the park, and the only bench to have originated outside of Disneyland, built years before the park was ever constructed or even envisioned.

I will take you to this bench before the end of this chapter. For now, know that this bench is for those of us who are leaders. This bench is for those of us interested in success. This bench belongs to those who believe they can change their lives and change their worlds by changing their thinking.

Every attraction in Disneyland tells a story. Our story begins with the story of this one park bench.

DREAMING BIG ON DADDY'S DAY

Once upon a time, Walt Disney sat on a park bench doing something he rarely, if ever, had time to do. *Nothing*. It was Saturday, and Saturdays were special in the Disney home because it was "Daddy's Day." Daddy's Day was the one day in the week when Walt would carve out time from his busy schedule to spend a few hours with his two little girls, Sharon and Diane. Each week, the three of them would head off together and find something to do. The family lived in Southern California, home to a multitude of museums, mountains, parks, and beaches.

On this particular Saturday, Walt took his girls to a place they knew well, Griffith Park. Griffith Park, the "Central Park of Los Angeles," allows both proximity and perspective. It is nestled high on a hill that sits between downtown L.A., Hollywood, and the Disney Studio in Burbank. There is a merry-go-round still there, built in 1926 and moved to Griffith Park in 1937, that Walt's two young girls loved to ride. Unlike most merry-go-rounds, all sixty-eight horses are "jumpers" with all four feet off the ground, and thus, they are highly prized by riders.

While Walt was sitting there doing nothing, whiling away the hour with only peanuts to keep him company, his head, like the merry-go-round in front of him, began to spin. "There should be a place," he thought. "A place where children and parents can have fun *together.*" And in that moment, the dream of Disneyland was born.

Have you ever done that? Have you ever been sitting somewhere, doing "nothing," and suddenly, an idea comes to you? An idea "pops" into your head, and your imagination begins to run wild with possibilities. Suddenly, you, like Walt, have a dream.

Walt Disney never stopped dreaming. If you are in the business of leadership and want to be successful, then you, like Walt, must *never* stop dreaming. When the idea of Disneyland came into his head and, ultimately, settled as a dream in his heart, Walt Disney was already one of the most successful people on the planet—a globally recognized household name. He had revolutionized animation, created Mickey Mouse, developed the first full-length animated motion picture (*Snow White and the Seven Dwarfs*), and built a major motion picture studio that was one of the most respected in all of Hollywood. Walt Disney was happily married, the father of two young girls, and a media mogul icon. Walt Disney had "arrived," and yet, despite all of these accomplishments, *Walt never stopped dreaming.* As authors Bill Capodagli and Lynn Jackson state in their book, *The Disney Way,* "Dreaming was the wellspring of Disney's creativity." And this dream, Disneyland, may very well have been his greatest dream of all.

LOOKING OUT THE WINDOW

In school, Walt Disney was, at best, an average student. According to Pat Williams and Jim Denney, in their book *How to Be Like Walt,* "His teachers complained that he was more inclined to daydreaming and drawing cartoons than completing assignments." I, too, have been designated as a dreamer. Paying attention in school wasn't always easy for me, either. My wife, Niki, likes to say that I am "educated beyond my intelligence." Some of my classmates who sat next to me in school and witnessed my inattention would no doubt concur!

Daydreaming became especially acute for me in graduate school. In a world before cellphones, laptops, or even the Internet, I still struggled to keep my focus. It did not take much to divert my attention away from the teacher. Any distraction became a doorway into my own world where my thoughts, dreams, and imagination roamed free of lectures and homework.

I once had a favorite professor who knew in advance that he was going to be away for a week's worth of classes. Rather than simply dismissing us for the week, he took the time and effort to have his lectures recorded for playback in the classroom. That way, the class could still meet, absorb the content, and not fall a full week behind. One afternoon during this week of videotaped lectures, the professor, having recorded everything well in advance, stopped his lecture and started shouting my name into the camera.

"Jeffrey! Jeffrey! You stop looking out that window right now!"

This amused my classmates to no end. Each whipped around to see my reaction. I, of course, missed all of this because I was, in fact, lost to the lecture as I dreamed longingly out the window. Too bad you can't earn a Ph.D. in dreaming!

Your first step to success is to do exactly what Walt did.

Nothing.

Take a Saturday and sit. Take a Sunday to think.

Take a weekend to DREAM.

I believe every successful person needs a park bench—that personal place where we can plan, set goals, and allow our imaginations to run wild. Your park bench is any place where you can begin to envision a bigger and better tomorrow.

The best gift a leader can give to his life, his family, and his organization is vision. Vision is an extension of the ability to dream. Walt himself said, "Money doesn't excite me—my ideas excite me."

We all have ideas. We all have dreams.

But making those dreams a reality involves taking the next step. The next step is vision. In his book *Disney and His Worlds*, Alan Bryman argues that Walt was a "serial visionary...someone who had big dreams about new ways of doing many things, whether it was making animated cartoons, designing amusement parks, or creating new approaches to urban living...."

LEFT BEHIND

IN *THE DISNEYLAND STORY*, DISNEYLAND historian Sam Gennawey writes that "Once upon a time, Walt Disney raised three wonderful children: Diane, Sharon, and Disneyland." I love this imagery because it tells us something important about our dreams.

You need to treat your dreams like you treat your children. Dreams, like children, don't raise themselves.

Like newborn babies, your dreams, your ideas, your goals, your ambitions, and your visions must be guarded and protected. You wouldn't leave a young child to sit alone on a park bench and "figure life out" on its own, so why would you do the same with your dreams?

You need a plan.

A plan for ensuring that your dreams get fed and your goals get nurtured. With the right amount of parenting, any dream, even a dream as big as Disneyland, can mature into reality.

A few years ago, Niki and I visited Disneyland over the busy Thanksgiving weekend. Aside from enjoying the attractions, we also did some browsing in the stores. Because we are Annual Passholders who frequent the park on a very regular basis, we no longer shop for souvenirs. On this day, however, I fell in love with a Disneyland sweater that I had never seen before. I tried it on and discovered that it fit me perfectly. Together, Niki and I made the rare decision to purchase it.

I left the store and took a seat on Main Street while Niki continued to shop. She walked up to me while I was lost in thought and asked whether I next wanted to ride the Disneyland Railroad. The railroad is one of my favorite attractions, so I readily agreed. While on board, I reached for my bag and realized I no longer had my new sweater. I had absentmindedly left it on my Main Street park bench. We waited until the train completed its twenty-minute "Grand Circle Tour" and returned us to the Main Street Station.

We raced over to the park bench, but it was empty. There wasn't a person, or sweater, in sight. We then checked with Lost and Found. The staff there had everything that had been lost in the park. Everything, of course, except my sweater. Lastly, on the recommendation of a cast member, we headed over to City Hall. Sadly, the staff there was also sans sweater.

We went home that night $75 poorer, with nothing to show for it, except maybe this lesson: Don't leave your thoughts, your ideas, your dreams, your goals, your vision—like my sweater— behind on a park bench.

Your thoughts matter.

Walt Disney changed his life, and our world, with an idea from a park bench. It was more than just a passing thought.

He didn't ignore his idea.

He didn't just stand up and walk away.

He trusted his vision, and over time, he took decisive action.

LEADERSHIP 101

THROUGHOUT HIS LIFE, WALT DISNEY followed his dreams and built his company as a visionary leader. His vision was so strong and his leadership skills so legendary that he represents one of the few business icons whose personality is inseparable from its brand. Other examples of this kind of transformational leadership include Steve Jobs at Apple, Richard Branson of Virgin, or Bill Gates at Microsoft.

According to Alan Bryman in *Disney and His Worlds,* Walt Disney embodied the concept of a charismatic leader as originally identified by German sociologist, philosopher, and political economist, Max Weber.

By definition, in order to be a leader, one must first have followers. A charismatic leader, however, must have followers who willingly follow him. Weber states, "By virtue of both the extraordinary qualities that followers attribute to the leader and the latter's mission, the charismatic leader is regarded by his or her followers with a mixture of reverence, unflinching dedication and awe."

Walt Disney provides us with what is really the lesson of Leadership 101. Our best leaders recognize that leadership has nothing to do with position or power. Your followers want to know where you are going to take them. Casting a compelling vision is critical to your success. Your followers need a reason to go where you are going. Leadership is *not* about managing things as they are today. Leadership is about transforming reality into *your* vision for a better tomorrow.

The dream for Disneyland was so powerful, and Walt's vision was so real, that he was able to recruit a whole new cast of followers to help make Disneyland real. This group of people came to be known as *Imagineers*. Imagineers were responsible for taking the ideas, thoughts, and visions of Walt's imagination, combining them with their own thoughts, ideas, and artistic talents, and then engineering them into reality.

This reality became Disneyland.

Disneyland stands today as a testament to the power of dreams. The power of thought. And the power of followers, like Imagineers, getting behind the power of vision.

POMP AND CIRCUMSTANCE(S)

My career in higher education began in August, 2000. Almost overnight, I was thrown into the role of both campus dean and full-time faculty member. Years later, I can still recall the first student I encountered in my newfound career. The campus was located on an Army post in Southeastern Arizona; it was part of a larger university system with campuses scattered around the United States.

Most of the students at our external campus sites, especially mine, had some sort of military background. As a result, the very first student who walked into my door on my first day on the job was a gentleman wearing the Army green. He held in his hand eight transcripts from eight different colleges. Collectively, he had managed to accumulate well over two hundred credit hours, but despite being a good student, he still held no degree.

Because I have three degrees but only two transcripts, this made zero sense to me. How could it be possible for someone to have eight transcripts, two hundred-plus credit hours, but never have actually graduated?

It was in that nonsensical moment that the vision for our campus crystallized. We live in a world where almost *anyone* can go to college and take a class. Having a college transcript is neither special nor unique.

But the goal is to *graduate*.

Our campus' mission would be to help students realize their dreams sooner rather than later. We existed for one reason and one reason only: to serve and assist students in their dreams to graduate!

Over the next nine years, a hyper-focus on this single mission allowed our campus to grow from the smallest school in Southeastern Arizona to the institution that issued more bachelor's degrees than any other. One of our proudest days was when a rival school closed up shop, claiming there "simply isn't a market" for schools in Southeastern Arizona. During this time, our campus also grew from being the smallest in the university system to the fifth largest. In terms of number of students versus available population, we were easily first.

This is the power of vision. This is the power of focusing on helping others realize their own dreams and their own goals.

Looking back on this story, I now know that I possessed a significant benefit that first day on the job. I was too stupid to know better.

No one had yet shown me what the politics of higher education really look like. No one had yet shared with me what a challenge it would be to grow a campus like one would grow a business. It took nine years, and if I had known on Day One everything it would take to get to year nine, I would have said, "No thanks." It is always tempting to stay where you are rather than risk taking the chances necessary to grow yourself, grow your company, and expand well beyond your comfort zone.

I suspect that if Walt Disney had any way of knowing what it was actually going to take to build Disneyland, he would have simply kept munching his peanuts and never would have given his idea a single second of additional thought.

Ignorance as a leader isn't the worst possible sin.

Who knows? You may just be stupid enough to try something never before considered or attempted.

CHOOSE YOUR DIRECTION

Disneyland's address in Anaheim, 1313 Harbor Boulevard, is exactly thirty-three miles from the merry-go-round in Griffith Park where Walt Disney first dreamed of a place where "children and parents could have fun together." From Disneyland's earliest beginnings, Walt always planned on putting his version of a merry-go-round in his Magic Kingdom. The King Arthur Carrousel that sits in the courtyard of Fantasyland, considered by many to be the heart of the park, has many notable features:

1. It is a carrousel, *not* a merry-go-round. What is the difference? A merry-go-round typically turns clockwise. Carrousels, however, usually spin counter-clockwise.

2. Note the spelling of carrousel with two r's versus the more traditional spelling with a single r, e.g., carousel. Both are correct with *carousel* being the English spelling of the original French word, *carrousel.*

3. Like its counterpart in Griffith Park, the King Arthur Carrousel also contains all jumpers. Walt went looking for something similar to what was in Griffith Park, only to learn that it was one-of-a-kind. Instead, he purchased a carousel in Toronto, Canada, and renovated it for greater capacity and to install all jumpers. Finding additional jumpers required a nationwide search and included horses from as far away as Coney Island, New York. Today, every horse is white, giving each guest the opportunity to be his or her own hero, riding high on a white steed.

Is your life going in the direction you wish for it to go? If not, know that you, and you alone, have the power to change course. Regardless of whether you wish to be a merry-go-round (going clockwise) or a revolutionary carrousel (going counter-clockwise), your direction is your decision.

Being your own hero and stepping onto your steed all begins with your thinking.

And your vision.

And most importantly, your *actions*!

SOUVENIR STOP

THIS IS THE FIRST OF many stops on our journey. Our Souvenir Stops are where we will pause, reflect, and develop takeaways from each experience. Don't just read through these sections. Take the time to write down your thoughts, your emotions, your actions, and most importantly, your commitments.

Like the shops in Disneyland, our stops will vary. By the end of this book, you should have a collection of "souvenirs" that will change your life and send you on your way to success. Let's get started.

FIND YOUR PARK BENCH—MOST OF this chapter focused on the importance of thinking. You value your thoughts by giving yourself time to think. Today, the Main Street Opera House, the first building ever constructed at Disneyland, houses the park bench where Walt first dreamed of Disneyland. The Opera House is also home to the Great Moments with Mr. Lincoln attraction. Abraham Lincoln once said, "You become what you think about."

On the line below, designate a space and a certain time (it can be as little as five minutes) each day where you focus on your thoughts. This can even be a daily form of meditation. Either way, your thoughts are where you start.

Place: ______________________________ Time: ________________

"Walt was the grand master of the vision."

— Imagineer Bob Gurr

Your Wild and Crazy Idea—Comedian and actor Steve Martin, the famous "Wild and Crazy Guy," began his career working at Disneyland. How fitting since most considered Walt Disney's idea for Disneyland just that, "Wild and Crazy!"

On the lines below, write down your crazy dream. What would you do? What could you accomplish? Who would you become if you knew, without question, that you could not fail?

____

____

____

Don't hold back.

Before writing anything down, reflect on the wise words of author Stephen Pressler in *Do the Work!*, "When an idea pops into our head and we think, 'No, this is too crazy,' that's the idea we want. 'When we think this notion is completely off the wall...should I take time to work on this?' the answer is yes."

"Walt was the greatest dreamer ever."

— How to Be Like Walt

GETTING YOUR HAND STAMPED

CONGRATULATIONS ON COMPLETING YOUR FIRST chapter! I know you will be coming back for more, however. Therefore, like a guest leaving Disneyland mid-day, I want to close this chapter, and every chapter, with a "handstamp" story. Guests leaving Disneyland mid-day are required to receive a handstamp on their hands. The handstamp is required for re-entry, and it always goes on your left hand.

These "handstamp" stories are meant to be memorable and, hopefully, they will leave a lasting impression, thus "stamping" the lesson from each chapter on you, the reader. The following story reminds us well of the importance of our thoughts and the power of vision.

Disneyland's counterpart, Walt Disney World in central Florida, is 2,504 miles away from Anaheim. Consisting of four theme parks, two water parks, thirty-three hotels, and multiple dining and shopping districts, Walt Disney World is the most popular vacation destination on the planet. Average annual attendance now surpasses seventeen million. Walt Disney World is also the largest single site employer in the United States, with over 66,000 cast members and counting.

Walt Disney World owes its existence to its smaller but older sibling, Disneyland, and the thinking of its creator, Walt Disney. As we will explore further, it too is a byproduct of Walt's ideas, dreams, and visions. Even though Walt Disney died on December 15, 1966 of lung cancer at the relatively young age of sixty-five and groundbreaking for Disney World didn't take place until a year later, 1967, the ideas were his.

In their book *How to Be Like Walt*, Pat Williams and Jim Denney share this story:

> Though Walt envisioned Walt Disney World in Florida, he died before it was built. On opening day in 1971, almost five years after his death, someone commented to Mike Vance, creative director of Walt Disney Studios, 'Isn't it too bad Walt Disney didn't live to see this?'
>
> 'He did see it,' Vance replied simply. 'That's why it's here.'

Now that you've received your handstamp, I'll see you soon in the next chapter.

PURSUING YOUR PASSION

*"Most of my life I have done what I wanted to do.
I have had fun on the job."*

DESTINATION DISNEYLAND

WALT DISNEY WAS FIFTY-THREE YEARS old the day he opened Disneyland. Despite his age, Walt's passion for pursuing some sort of park was anything but a mid-life crisis. Biographers speculate that Walt's father, Elias, initially sparked his son's interest in amusement parks. Walt grew up hearing his father's stories about his time as a day laborer at the 1893 Columbian Exposition in Chicago. This event, celebrating the 400th anniversary of Christopher Columbus' expedition, gave America the Ferris wheel, the first all-electric kitchen, and other innovations such as Cracker Jacks. Twenty-seven million people visited the World's Fair in a mere six months. The event left an indelible mark on both the world and Elias Disney.

Elias' stories about the World's Fair stood in stark contrast to his otherwise strict, stern, and humorless personality. Walt loved his father and honored him with a "Window on Main Street," recognized as the highest level of tribute in the park. The "Elias Disney, Contractor, Est. 1895" window sits just above the Emporium Department Store.

Nonetheless, young Walt recoiled at growing up under such a rigid and unimaginative man. Amusement parks represent escape. Elias' stories about his youthful Exposition escapades were in contrast to the middle-aged father Walt knew. Those stories provided Walt with a passion for entertainment. They also ignited in him a desire to leave his current situation and step into the world of his dreams and limitless imagination.

Eventually, Elias moved the family from Chicago to Marceline, Missouri. Later, they moved to Kansas City, Missouri, where Walt first saw an actual amusement park—two in fact. The first, Fairmount Park, sat just two blocks from where Walt lived. According to Williams and Denney in *How to Be Like Walt,* Ruth, Walt's sister, remembered that she and Walt "would peer through the fence, longing to enter."

The second Kansas City park, Electric Park, was one of America's largest. In retrospect, it is obvious that this park left a passionate impression on young Walt. The similarities are striking. Electric Park included thrill rides, music, spectacular nighttime fireworks, and, most significantly, a steam-powered train surrounding the park's perimeter. In an America where only a third of the population could access electricity, Electric Park was most noted for lighting up the night with more than 100,000 lightbulbs a number that's illuminatingly identical to what exists today on Main Street in Disneyland. Perhaps Walt was recalling his passion for Electric Park when he said, "Disneyland has that *thing*—the imagination and the feeling of happy excitement—I knew when I was a kid."

Electric Park burned to the ground in 1925. Walt Disney had long since left for California, but another Walter, Walter Cronkite, the not-yet-famous newscaster, was there to chronicle it firsthand, at the age of nine. In his autobiography, *Walter Cronkite, A Reporter's Life,* he wrote:

> Our hill overlooked, a half dozen blocks away, Electric Park, one of Kansas City's early amusement parks. One night after closing, it burned in a spectacular fire. The Ferris wheel seemed to turn as the flames climbed up its sides. The grease caught fire on the

> two parallel tracks of the Greyhound Racer roller coaster, and twin blazes raced up and down with the speed of the cars that once followed the tortuous circuit. The fun house collapsed in a terrible shower of sparks.

People had a preview of *Disneyland* at the December 21, 1937 premiere of *Snow White and the Seven Dwarfs* at Los Angeles' Carthay Circle Theatre. Walt themed the front of the theatre with life-size mockups of the dwarfs' cottage, a forest scene, mushrooms, and a mill with a running waterfall. According to Williams and Denney in *How to Be Like Walt*, that evening, Walt told one of his animators, "Someday, I want to build a park for kids to play in—a place with fantasy cottages like these, all scaled down to a child's size."

As the years passed, Walt's passion for a park filled his imagination with a variety of possible ideas and concepts. At one point, he sketched a "Mickey Mouse Park," which would be located on the perimeter of the Disney Studio in Burbank and across the street from Forest Lawn Mortuary (dubbed by Disney archivist Dave Smith, as "the Theme Park for Shut-Ins"). Walt envisioned a place that was clean, well-run, and included a merry-go-round and Disney-themed rides. His drawings included what we now recognize as a mini-version of Main Street and a mini-version of Frontierland. Park patrons would be able to tour the studio and ride a scale-model steam train that would transport them from the park to the studio and back. An internal Disney memo, written by Walt himself, reveals further detail: "In the park will be benches, a bandstand, drinking fountains, trees, and shrubs. It will be a place for people to sit and rest; mothers and grandmothers can watch over small children at play. I want it to be very relaxing, cool, and inviting."

However, fearing traffic and crowds, "Beautiful Downtown Burbank" wanted nothing to do with Disney's dream. According to *The Disneyland Story*, one local lawmaker proclaimed, "We don't want the carny atmosphere in Burbank! We don't want people falling in the river, or merry-go-rounds squawking all day long." This protest came down in Walt's favor because his dream soon became bigger than what his few acres of studio space could accommodate. As he began to plan riverboats, pirate ships, rivers, and a castle, he quickly realized he was going to need "a bigger moat."

Big dreams require big canvases.

Undeterred, in 1953, Walt commissioned the Stanford Research Group to help him find the best location for his "Disneyland." Walt wanted flat land, a blank canvas on which he could construct, on his own natural stage, storybook versions of lakes, rivers, and mountains. He paid the Stanford Research Group $250,000 for its study, and they came back with four recommendations. The Ball Road Subdivision in the then little-known town of Anaheim was their number one choice. Groundbreaking would take place in July 1954, and the park would open exactly one year later, July 17, 1955.

Years later, Walt reflected back on Anaheim, "In those days it was all flat land-no rivers, no mountains, no castles or rocket ships-just orange groves and a few walnut trees."

Isn't it funny how life works? Today, when you think of Walt Disney, you naturally associate him with the parks, lands, and worlds he created. Yet, Disneyland actually represents a relatively small percentage of his life and career.

Disneyland is such a special place. It is the *only* park that bears Walt's footprints. Walt didn't live long enough to walk in Walt Disney World, or any of the other international parks that bear his name: Tokyo Disneyland, Disneyland Paris, Hong Kong Disneyland, and Shanghai Disneyland.

Walt's passion for building the perfect park was so great that it outlived his mortal body.

When you look back on Walt's life, his father's influence is obvious. He was fueled by his father's stories about the World's Fair. You can see flashes of the future as early as Walt's excitement about Electric Park in Kansas City. His proposed Mickey Mouse Park, across the street from the studio, was a close facsimile of the future Disneyland, but Burbank never allowed it. Walt's dream is all the better for it.

LIVING LIFE UNDECLARED

In my career, I have the privilege of working with "undeclared" college students, young people who have yet to pick their majors. It is common for these students to come in during the first semester of their freshman year and fear they are already behind. They don't yet know what they want to be when they grow up. They look at their friends and peers with majors and immediately feel "less than." Everyone else has it figured out. Everyone else knows who he is. Everyone else knows what she wants to do...for the *rest of their lives*. Imagine earning an "F" before your first day of class. This is what it feels like to be an undeclared student.

In order to reassure these students, I share this reality: up to 70 percent of all college students change their majors, many as often as three times before graduation. In truth, we are almost all "undeclared." My incoming freshmen know it, but it takes several semesters, or the remainder of our lives, for the rest of us to figure this out.

Clearly, Walt Disney lived his life undeclared. Was he an ambulance driver? An artist? An actor? A cartoonist? An animator? A bankrupt businessman? An entrepreneur? A voice-over artist? A full-length animated film producer? A studio movie mogul? A live-action film director? An amusement park operator? An urban planner?

The answer is "Yes!"

Walt was a man of passion. He pursued his dreams with persistence, and he trusted that the right results would follow. In turn, he lived an unimaginable life that is the envy of many.

Success is like the architecture in Mickey's Toontown at Disneyland; there are no straight lines. Instead, success swoops, swerves, and veers off in directions that seem to head nowhere. As Steve Jobs, who attended college but never graduated, shared with the 2005 graduating class at Stanford University:

> ...you can't connect the dots looking forward; you can only connect them looking backward. So you have to trust that the dots will somehow connect in your future. You have to trust in something—your gut, destiny, life, karma, whatever. This approach has never let me down, and it has made all the difference in my life.

In his book, *The Art of Work*, Jeff Goins, whose writing helped ignite my passion for writing this book, puts the following perspective on pursuing your passions:

> The experience of finding your calling [passion] is both mysterious and practical. It takes effort but also seems to happen to you at times. What I've come to understand is that finding your purpose is more of a path than a plan: it involves unexpected twists and turns that at times look like accidents but actually are a part of the process.

TEACHING THE HISTORY OF DISNEYLAND

AFTER MANY TWISTS AND TURNS, my journey finally allowed me to do what I knew I wanted to do as early as middle school: teach U.S. history. If you were bored in school by history, I apologize. The problem isn't that history is boring; you probably had boring teachers. People are rarely bored by passion. My passion keeps students awake, even those taking a 7:00 a.m. course.

Walt Disney was destined to build Disneyland. Ask anyone who knew me growing up, and he will tell you I was destined to teach history. Now, you may wonder how teaching history eventually led to teaching a course on the history of Disneyland?

It started one afternoon when I was lecturing during a U.S. history course on the decade of the 1950s. Naturally, it is my belief that any American history course that covers the 1950s should include the subject of Disneyland. The park opened in the middle month of the middle year of that iconic decade, July 17, 1955. It was an event that resonated with the culture of the 1950s, combining leisure time, television, music, and an innate desire to "get away from it all." It has been iconic Americana ever since.

When I began teaching about Disneyland, student interest soared even further. Questions came rapid fire as my students responded to the story about the park's opening. Out of curiosity, I asked my students, "How many of you have been to Disneyland?" Every hand (more than sixty!) shot up. This shouldn't have been a surprise, since the university is only thirty-three miles away from Main Street, U.S.A.

I then asked a more important question, "How many of you were so young that you don't remember the first time you went to Disneyland?" Seventy-five percent of those very same hands shot up.

They don't know, I realized. *They've never heard the story!*

This generation has never known a world *without* Disneyland. The park has always been right there, in their own backyard. They don't know the story. They take it for granted. The story of Disneyland is a success story that, in my opinion, every student should know. It epitomizes what is great about America and sets the excellence bar high.

Secretly, I've always wanted to work as a Disneyland tour guide. This course was my chance. By connecting the dots, I was able to marry my passion for history with my love for Disneyland. A brand-new course was born, "The History of Disneyland." When my students and I go to the park, I take on the persona of "Dr. Disneyland" and give the class a guided tour. Students bring friends and family. I am sharing my passion, so the more the merrier!

On this tour, we see Walt's passion for building Disneyland, a passion that stayed alive throughout his life, not only as he added to Disneyland, but even as he planned another park. According to *How to Be Like Walt*, the night before Walt died in 1966, his brother, Roy, visited him. Roy watched Walt stare at the ceiling tiles over his deathbed and lay out parks and roads. For Walt, the tiles represented a grid of the property where he was developing his biggest dream, Walt Disney World, an amusement park 150 times the size of Disneyland.

PASSION AND PERSPECTIVE

DEATH, OR AT LEAST THE prospect of death, has the power of perspective. As a brain tumor survivor, I experienced that morbid moment when you first realize that you aren't going to be here forever.

During the first week of May, the same year I finally started my History of Disneyland class, I had a long-sought appointment with a neurologist. For years, I had suffered from severe headaches that had become acute over the past few months. When Niki and I walked into the neurologist's office and saw my MRI on the screen, we immediately knew there was trouble. A six-year-old child could spot the tumor growing on my brain. This wasn't rocket science, just brain surgery. The doctor immediately referred me to a neurosurgeon at Cedars-Sinai in Los Angeles.

A few days later, we drove to Los Angeles for the scheduled appointment. In the interim, I had managed to delude myself into believing this really wasn't a big deal. My thoughts careened from "The doctors are only going to need to monitor this," to "Worst-case scenario, they will operate in the morning, and I will be back in the classroom that afternoon." In the future, when you see your first outpatient brain surgery clinic, remember, you read it here first.

We were the first appointment that morning at Cedars-Sinai, and we waited patiently for the doctor to call us in. When the polite receptionist offered us water or coffee, I couldn't help but think, "Man, your job sucks. Nobody comes in here for good news and you benignly offer coffee or water?"

When the neurosurgeon met with us, he read my MRI and promptly pronounced, "That's got to come out."

Okay, so much for my self-prescribed "wait and see" approach. I took a deep breath and asked, "When?"

He replied, "How about Tuesday?"

I've ridden every attraction at Disneyland. I haven't missed anything. There is one ride, however, that I try to avoid as much as possible. I rarely, if ever, take a spin on the Mad Tea Party's teacups. However, instantly the doctor's office became a Fantasyland "Dark Ride," incorporating the teacups' motion. The room would not stop spinning. After a few minutes, I was able to gather myself enough to utter a recognizable response.

"That's not going to happen."

"What's not going to happen?" the doctor asked.

"Tuesday. Tuesday isn't happening. You can't operate on me on Tuesday because I have class."

He explained to me that the day of the week didn't matter much because the recovery time, regardless, was a minimum of six weeks. Once again, I rarely ride the teacups and certainly never back-to-back, but there went the room all over again.

I told the doctor he wasn't going to be operating on me that Tuesday, or any Tuesday, in the near future. Of course, he wanted to know what I was doing on Tuesdays that was so important that I needed to postpone my own brain surgery. I explained to him that I, too, am a doctor—a university professor who teaches during the summer. Our summer session had just begun. I added that this wasn't just *any* summer, and certainly not just *any* class. This was my dream. My passion. I wasn't going to throw away a year's worth of work or walk away from the opportunity of a lifetime. If we cancelled the class, it might never show up on the schedule again.

I'm not sure what kind of curriculum he imagined. Perhaps molecular biology?

Aghast, the doctor allowed me to delay the surgery until July 24, a Thursday.

Over the months of that endless summer, friends and colleagues often asked how I could be so careless. The idea that I would delay brain surgery just so I could teach a Mickey Mouse class about a theme park seemed trivial to most people. They either didn't get Disneyland, or they didn't understand that I wanted to use the popularity of Disneyland as a vehicle for teaching stories about success and lessons on life and leadership. This is my passion. A not-so-little brain tumor and a know-it-all neurosurgeon weren't going to shut me down before I ever really had the chance to get started.

As a historian, I was ultimately empowered by the words of Roman Emperor Marcus Aurelius: "Stop whatever you're doing for a moment and ask yourself: Am I afraid of death because I won't be able to do this anymore?"

I did not want to die with my dream, my passion, my story still inside me.

"There is no greater agony than bearing an untold story inside of you."

— Maya Angelou

SOUVENIR STOP

It isn't easy. We all want our passion, purpose, and pathway to success to be clear and obvious. We want the entire route illuminated before we start. Instead, it is like a cross-country journey by car—at night. We can only see a few feet in front of us at a time. Nonetheless, we keep driving forward. We keep making progress. We keep connecting the dots and trust that the few feet of roadway that the headlights are showing us are taking us in the right direction.

In a "TED Talk" video seen more than eight million times, Richard St. John shares his "Eight Secrets of Success." Number one is passion. To help you find yours, I encourage you to explore the following:

Go Back to Start—The theme of this chapter is that Walt was destined to build Disneyland. Of course, we can only see this when we look *backwards*. Look back on your life, and connect the dots. Follow the breadcrumbs (even if most of them have been eaten), and see where they take you. Find anything interesting? What kind of pattern(s) emerge? Who were you destined to be?

I have a picture in my head from my childhood. It is the image of me sitting on the floor playing with an electric train set. The entire track circled a multi-piece puzzle of Disneyland that my mom had purchased on her first visit to the park in the early 1960s, a few years before I was born. Needless to say, that scene makes more sense to me at age fifty than it ever could have at five.

What I knew at age five was that I was having fun. Children often work out life's problems through play. I believe adults should do the same. After all, if you aren't having fun, what's the point? As Walt Disney himself said, "Disneyland is not just another amusement park. It's unique, and I want to keep it that way. Besides, you don't work for a dollar—you work to create and have fun."

Find Out What Excites You—Passion isn't about a job, a career, or even a purpose. Passion is about excitement. In *Talk Like Ted: The 9 Public-Speaking Secrets of the World's Great Minds,* Carmine Gallo defines passion as: "a positive, intense feeling that you experience for something that is profoundly meaningful for you as an individual."

Know that it is okay for your passion to be highly personal. People, including his wife and brother, thought Walt was crazy for wanting to build an amusement park. I've gotten more than my share of stares when I explain that I teach a college-level course on Disneyland. If you aren't excited about it, then how can you expect anyone else to be? Live your life with the following motto, and know that your passion is more powerful than your fear: It is easier to tame a zealot than to pump life into a cadaver.

"Walt was excited about...his theme park. When he was excited about something, his excitement fired up everyone around him. That's how he sold his dreams."

— *How to Be Like Walt*

Put Your Passion in Perspective—Speaking of fear, what are you afraid of missing if you die? What would you do if money were no concern? What will others miss about you after you are gone? You don't have to figure it all out today, but I do want you to get started—*now*. None of us has forever. Before you head to the next world, *this* world needs you, your dreams. your ideas, and your passion.

"We are all born to be who we are. Walt Disney was a genetically unique individual who was born to be himself. His job, and ours as well, is to finish the job on earth that we were created for."

— Ray Bradbury

GETTING YOUR HAND STAMPED

Remember how Walt needed enough land to build his dream, a dream that included castles, jungle cruises, rocket ships, and mountains? Once he purchased his 160 acres in Anaheim, he had to clear his canvas of its orange groves and walnut trees. He did, however, wish to save some trees. Trees destined to stay, he marked red. The ones he wanted cleared, he marked green. Then he promptly hired a color-blind bulldozer operator who couldn't tell the difference; he cleared everything.

Finding your passion is a process. Passion isn't unique this way. Everything in life is a process. No matter what your canvas might look like today, know that it has a purpose. Where you see red, others might see green. Where you see green, others might see purple. In the end, it doesn't matter. You can still build on it. Be excited about your dreams, ideas, and future.

Trust the process.

Most importantly, trust your passion.

LISTENING TO YOUR "WALTER" EGO

"The life and ventures of Mickey Mouse have been closely bound up with my own personal and professional life. It is understandable that I should have sentimental attachment for the little personage who played so big a part in the course of Disney Productions.... He still speaks for me and I still speak for him."

IT ALL STARTED WITH A MOUSE

Walt Disney was fond of reminding people that we should never lose sight of the fact that it all started with a mouse. I think it is safe to say that no one has forgotten about Mickey Mouse. Whenever you walk into one of Disney's theme parks, the image of Mickey is everywhere. The floral Mickey is at the center of Disneyland's entrance—a favorite picture spot, especially for first-time visitors. This cherished piece of luscious landscaping is replanted six to nine times each year. Colors rotate throughout the calendar to represent seasonal scenes, inviting local park guests to return again and again throughout the year.

For children, seeing Mickey the first time on their inaugural visit is a video highlight every parent wants to record. Some of these sightings are serendipitous; others are carefully crafted via character meet and greets that are well-timed and strategically located throughout the park. Today, both Mickey and Minnie Mouse have their own homes in Mickey's Toontown, an area added to the park in 1993. Since its inception, Disneyland has been Mickey's domain, and he remains the dominant character in the world crafted by his creator, Walt.

Today, "Hidden Mickeys" are also a fan favorite, especially for the million-plus locals in Southern California who hold annual passes and visit the park multiple times in any given year (or even week). A "Hidden Mickey" is a representation of Mickey Mouse that Imagineers have placed, subtly, in the park. The Hidden Mickeys are of various sizes and forms, and guests turn locating them into a game, seeing who can spot the most Mickeys hiding in queues, props, attractions, restaurants, shops, and even streetlamps. My personal favorite is the "notso-hidden Mickey" hanging above the "reverse waterfall" on Pirates of the Caribbean. Just as guests prepare to disembark from their boats and exit the ride, you pass under three wooden barrels held up by rope. The barrels are buoyed with two barrels on top (Mickey's ears) and one barrel below (Mickey's face). Online fans "guesstimate" there are well over 300 Hidden Mickeys inside Disneyland. Thirty-three of these are within New Orleans Square alone, including the face placed in Pirates of the Caribbean.

THE BIRTH OF MICKEY MOUSE

WHILE WE CERTAINLY HAVEN'T FORGOTTEN Mickey Mouse, most people don't realize that Mickey Mouse almost didn't happen. After Walt arrived in Los Angeles from Kansas City in 1923, with one suit and all of forty dollars, the first successful character in the newly formed Disney studio was Oswald the Rabbit. Oswald brought Walt his first real success and his first real profits. Toward the end of that decade, Oswald was popular enough, and Walt confident enough, that he traveled, by train, all the way to New York City to negotiate a more favorable distribution deal with Universal.

The deal never happened.

Walt quickly learned that neither he, nor the Disney studio, even owned the rights to Oswald. To make matters worse, Universal was already in the process of stealing not just Oswald the Rabbit but the very animators who had helped make Disney and Oswald so successful.

It was a long ride home.

Knowing that he would need to come up with something fast if he were going to save the studio, Walt remembered a little mouse who had befriended him in his small office back in Kansas City. He began drawing the rodent from memory, showed him to his wife, Lillian, and proposed the name "Mortimer." Lillian objected to Mortimer, sensing, correctly, that the moniker was "too heavy." They came up with Mickey instead. Years later, Walt's brother, Roy, reflecting on Mickey Mouse, would say, "Thank God we didn't name him Mortimer." Walt's own recollections are as follows:

> Why did I choose a mouse…? Principally because I needed a small animal. I couldn't use a rabbit, because there already was a rabbit on the screen [no doubt a reference to the lost Oswald]. So I decided upon a mouse, as I have always thought they were very interesting little creatures. At first I decided to call him Mortimer Mouse, but changed his name to Mickey as the name has a more friendly sound…. While returning from a visit to New York, I plotted out the first story.

Mickey Mouse would go on to be the most successful cartoon character in history and the foundation for what we know today to be the Disney Empire. As Bob Thomas observed in *Walt Disney: An American Original,* "a man gave birth to a mouse. The mouse built the man an empire."

WHY MICKEY MOUSE WORKS

At his core, Mickey works because of his simplicity. Animator Ub Iwerks, one of Walt's few cartoonists who was not stolen away in the Universal double-cross, took responsibility for providing Mickey with form and movement. According to Walt:

> Mickey had to be simple. We had to push out seven hundred feet of film every two weeks. His head was a circle with an oblong circle for a snout. The ears were also circles so they could be drawn the same, no matter how he turned his head. His body was like a pear, and he had a long tail. His legs were pipestems, and we stuck them in large shoes to give him the look of a kid wearing his father's shoes. We didn't want him to have mouse hands, because he was supposed to be more human. So we gave him gloves. Five fingers seemed like too much on such a little figure, so we took away one. There was just one less finger to animate. To provide a little detail, we gave him the two-button pants. There was no mouse hair, or any other frills that would slow down animation.

The decision to limit Mickey to four digits instead of five has saved millions of dollars in animation costs over the years. Millions that Walt would need one day to build Disneyland.

While Ub focused on the drawings, Walt provided Mickey with his whimsical personality. Originally, Mickey was intended to be an animated version of the perpetually popular Charlie Chaplin. In one sense, Walt succeeded in that goal. According to John Lasseter, Chief Creative Officer of Walt Disney and Pixar Animation Studios, "There was a period of time when they estimated the two biggest stars in Hollywood were Charlie Chaplin and Mickey Mouse." But most will agree that the resulting Mickey Mouse was more like Walt Disney than Charlie Chaplin. Most associate Walt with Mickey because it was Walt who provided Mickey with his original voice. But the connection is much, much deeper. Biographer Bob Thomas writes:

> Both Walt and Mickey had an adventurous spirit, a sense of rectitude, an admitted lack of sophistication, a boyish ambition to excel...both clung to the old-fashioned notion of remaining steadfast to one sweetheart.

During the Depression, President Roosevelt ordered that Mickey Mouse cartoons be shown at the White House. Mickey Mouse was such an American cultural icon that as early as 1935, years before the outbreak of World War II, Adolf Hitler banned Mickey Mouse cartoons from German theatres. His "reasoning":

> Mickey Mouse is the most miserable ideal ever revealed.... Healthy emotions tell every independent young man and every honorable youth that the dirty and filth-covered vermin, the greatest bacteria carrier in the animal kingdom, cannot be the ideal type of animal.... Away with Jewish brutalization of the people! Down with Mickey Mouse! Wear the Swastika Cross!

By contrast, on D-Day, Allied soldiers used the password "Mickey Mouse" to distinguish between enemy and friendly forces. History has come to interpret Mickey Mouse as an indomitable spirit, resourceful, and, as a medal given to Walt by the League of Nations, testifies, a "symbol of universal good will." A symbol of universal good will? Why, that sounds like Walt Disney himself! Animator Frank Thomas said, "There's a special sense in which Walt truly *was* Mickey—and Mickey *was* Walt." In fact, after his death, Walt's wife, Lillian, remarked, "Whenever I see Mickey Mouse I have to cry. Because he reminds me so much of Walt."

WHOM DO YOU TRUST?

Mickey Mouse was Walt Disney's alter ego. How fun! Wouldn't it be awesome to have an alter ego to speak for you from time to time?

To say what you cannot say? To do what you cannot do? Wouldn't it be amazing if your own inner voice had an outlet, a character like Mickey Mouse, who could go on adventures, fall in love, be the focus of worldwide adoration, and yet still be safe and secure inside an animation cell?

If you and your ideas are destined for success, then you need to learn to listen to your "Walter" ego. Just as your ideas matter, so too does your instinct and your inner voice.

Think about it.

Leaders form teams via the transaction of trust. Trust is earned. By the same token, you cannot give what you do not have. If you do not trust yourself, your inner voice, or your "Walter ego," then why should anyone trust you?

I am proud to say that I, too, have a "Walter" ego. As early as the first century, the Roman philosopher Cicero wrote of humans having a second self, which he described as anyone or anything you can call a "trusted friend." My second self or "Walter" ego isn't a world famous character like Mickey Mouse. But he is a character.

Back in the 1980s, the Ganza toy company created a line of puppet dogs called "Wrinkles." I purchased one in January 1987. I originally wanted to name him Aleph, the first letter in the Hebrew alphabet, since I was studying Hebrew at the time. Eventually, I settled on a much simpler and softer appellation, Albert.

Albert has been my second self and trusted friend for nearly three decades now. Anyone who really knows me also knows Albert. I consider him my son. So much so that my *real* daughter, Bethany, grew up believing, at least during her younger years, that Albert was, in fact, her brother. Today, Bethany works as an investigative reporter in Las Vegas where she separates fact from fiction.

A coincidence? Albert thinks not!

Albert will say what isn't safe for me to say. He will think thoughts that are separate and apart from me, thoughts that simply would not exist if he didn't. Albert populates his own world with his own ideals and his own values. In other words, Albert makes it safe for me to have an inner voice and to speak my mind without reserve from time to time.

We all have an inner voice.

Too often, our competing inner critic stifles this voice. Our inner critic doesn't dare risk ridicule from the outside world. For me, Albert makes it safe to speak, and I simply cannot imagine my world without him.

It doesn't take much imagination to imagine you, my reader, worrying right now.

Alter Ego? Walter Ego? Mickey Mouse? Albert?

Strange? Yes!

Crazy? Not so much!

Few of us would argue that Walt was not a genius. And we can readily recognize that his kingdom was, in fact, built on the back of a mouse. But let's face facts. Mickey Mouse isn't real. Neither is Albert (as much as it pains me to admit). Mickey Mouse is simply an extension of Walt Disney. His second self. A trusted friend. Trusted not just by Walt but by the entire world.

Where would we be today if Walt had not felt safe and secure enough to extend himself through Mickey? Orange County, California would look a lot different. Few of us, I imagine, would have ever heard of Orlando, Florida, or certainly, have ever had a compelling reason to go there. Disney legend, Marty Sklar, tells the story of how he and other Disney executives were responsible for selling the EPCOT concept throughout the country during the late 1970s—an era when public trust, following Vietnam and Watergate, was at an all-time low. The idea of EPCOT was difficult to convey, but without corporate sponsors, the project was dead. In his biography, *Dream It! Do It!*, Sklar states that feedback on the initial ideas of EPCOT included the following: "The public does not trust what industry, government, and even academia tell them. The public *does* trust Mickey Mouse."

VILLAINOUS VOICES

EVERY GOOD STORY NEEDS A hero. The challenge is that you cannot have a hero without some sort of villain, and that's okay because as Jon Acuff says in his book *Start: Punch Fear in the Face, Escape Average, and Do Work that Matters:* "stories without dragons are boring." Mickey Mouse had to battle his arch-nemesis, the now politically incorrect Pegleg Pete. Originally a bear, over time, Pete evolved into an anthropomorphic cat. Cats, of course, are natural predators of mice. Just as we view Mickey as Walt's alter ego, Pegleg Pete is perceived as a symbol of Walt's own battles with adversity.

The villain to your inner voice is an enemy you know well. It is your inner critic, the voice that drowns out your dreams and desires. You know the dialogue well:

"Who are you to do that?" "You're not good enough!"

"What do you know about what you are trying to accomplish?" "It better be perfect or you shouldn't even bother!"

"Why would anyone ever care about that?"

Sound familiar? Exactly. And the bigger your dream, the bigger your dragon.

Walt's biggest dream was his "Florida Project." We know it today as Walt Disney World, 150 times the size of the original Disneyland. Unfortunately, Walt didn't live to see this dream to fruition. When he died in 1966, the baton passed to his older brother, Roy. Ground breaking in Florida took place in 1967, and crews completed construction on the world's second Magic Kingdom four years later. Roy was on hand to dedicate and open Walt Disney World on October 1, 1971. Of course, the rest of Walt's family was there as well. The dedication is described in *How to Be Like Walt*:

> As Roy went to the platform to give his dedication speech, he stopped and looked around as if something was missing. John

> Hench, who was nearby, heard Roy quietly tell an aide, 'Would you go find Mickey for me? We don't have Walt anymore, and Mickey's the nearest thing to Walt we have left.' Moments later, Mickey Mouse joined Roy on the platform.

We all have an inner voice. And within your inner voice resides your true genius. This is where your true self lives. Who are you? What do you want to do? Where do you want to go? What is it you aspire to accomplish? The answers to all of these questions echo in the sound of our own inner voice.

If you want to change your world—if you want to lead a better life—then I implore you to listen and trust your "Walter" ego. Get good with your second self. Allow it to be your true and trusted friend.

SOUVENIR STOP

In the next chapter, we will explore the importance of story. For now, just imagine your life as an ongoing narrative, filled with a cast of characters, plot, conflict, and resolution. If this sounds like your real life, it is! Let's do some character development.

First, we need to work on the heroes in your story. Your heroes are, of course, you and your alter ego. Your alter ego is there; trust me. Like Mickey, he might be hidden, but his silhouette is scattered throughout the landscape of your life. Ask yourself the following questions:

1. What is your alter ego's name? (Be careful not to make it too heavy, e.g., Mortimer or Aleph.)

___

___

2. What are its physical attributes? Be as specific as possible. Male or female? Short or tall? Slim or portly? (Albert could lose a few

pounds.) What color is his hair? What color are her eyes? Fill out the details as if your alter ego might one day actually be animated.

---

3. What kinds of clothes does your alter ego prefer? Remember, Mickey started out poor and simple, but today he has a closet full of clothes and costumes. For the record, Albert has a strong preference for corduroy.

---

4. Most importantly, what are the personality traits of your alter ego? How do they vary from your own personality? How can these traits enhance and enable who you are and what you wish to accomplish? You want your alter ego to be more fascinating than yourself. How is she smarter? How is he sexier? Does your alter ego have a mean streak? Know that you are developing a soulmate. You are creating a lifelong friend who will come alongside you and serve as a hero, a partner, and a sidekick to your success.

Finally, we need to name your villain, your evil, inner critic. You probably don't need much help here because, if you are like most, your villainous voice is no doubt *already* well-developed. Picture some of the various villains that complete the catalogue of characters in the Disney archives, e.g., The Big Bad Wolf (*Three Little Pigs*), Maleficent (*Sleeping Beauty*), Captain Hook (*Peter Pan*), Cruella de Vil (*101 Dalmatians*), Ursula the Sea Witch (*The Little Mermaid*), Scar (*The Lion King*), or Mother Gothel (*Tangled*). Remember, these evil individuals are always vanquished in the end; your inner critic can be slain as well.

GETTING YOUR HAND STAMPED

IN DISNEYLAND'S CENTRAL PLAZA, BETWEEN the end of Main Street and Sleeping Beauty Castle, stands the "Partners Statue." This statue features both Walt Disney and Mickey Mouse. Walt is raising his right arm and pointing south toward Main Street and the Train Station. With his left arm, Walt is standing hand-in-hand with his alter ego, Mickey Mouse. Sculpted by Blaine Gibson, the same Imagineer who took the sculpting lead for the Abraham Lincoln audio-animatronic figure in Great Moments with Mr. Lincoln, the park unveiled the statue in November, 1993—the 65th anniversary of the release of the first Mickey Mouse cartoon, "Steamboat Willie," and Mickey's Mouse's official birthday.

I interviewed a former Disneyland Princess, Chelsea, regarding the statue. She shared with me that in Traditions, the orientation program for all new cast members, she had heard several statue stories. First, there is a "Hidden Mickey" on the ring Walt is wearing on the hand pointing down Main Street. Secondly, the statue allows Walt to realize one of his rare, unfulfilled wishes. In real life, Walt was 5' 10", but he always wanted to be two inches taller. Sure enough, Walt is 6' in the Partners statue and rises to 6' 5" when placed on the pedestal. Way to go, Walt!

Most significantly, the Partners Statue is symbolic of the symbiotic relationship between Walt and Mickey. Neither could accomplish anything without the other. Walt and Mickey are facing the park's entrance as if Walt, proud of their lifelong partnership, is saying to Mickey, "Look at all the happy people who have come to visit us today."

I encourage you never to lose sight of your alter ego, your inner voice, a true and trusted friend. Like Walt and Mickey, form a lifelong partnership with it. Imagine surveying the street at the end of your dream, your goal, your accomplishment, and welcoming all of the happiness that will accompany its arrival.

TELLING STORIES

"I'm a storyteller. Of all the things I've ever done, I'd like to be remembered as a storyteller."

WHAT WE NEED MOST

DISNEYLAND SPEAKS A UNIVERSAL LANGUAGE. Before you jump to conclusions, don't assume this language is love or even happiness. At Walt's Magic Kingdom, the lingua franca, or language of the realm, is story. We know Disneyland as "The Happiest Place on Earth," but those who recognize the significance of story might well call it "The Most Necessary Place on Earth." Absurd? Consider first the words of novelist Phillip Pullman, "after nourishment, shelter and companionship, stories are the thing we need most in the world."

In Disneyland, Walt met our felt need for story. The emphasis on story is what sets Disneyland apart. Amusement parks existed before Disneyland, and other companies have constructed theme parks since. But it was Disneyland that started the story of using narrative in public places to connect with people in powerful, emotional, and memorable ways. Disneyland stands above the rest because it stood first on the shoulders of story.

In order to appreciate fully what Walt set out to do, you need to approach Disneyland like Americans approached movie theatres during the first half of the twentieth century. First and foremost, Walt Disney was a storyteller, and he spent years telling his stories in the grand theatres that dominated the landscape during his career. In Hollywood, Walt's own backyard, theatres, such as Grauman's Egyptian and Chinese theatres, were elaborately themed and provided Walt the backdrop for his vision of Disneyland. According to a recent article on the Disney fan site Micechat, "While most projects had architects doing the designing, Walt Disney relied on his staff of motion picture designers. He envisioned his park as one big movie set, with forced perspective and transitions such as one might see in a movie."

How did he go about doing that? Let's go to Disneyland and find out:

Outer Lobby: Walt purchased 160 acres in Anaheim, but the park only topped out at around 100 acres. What happened to the other sixty? Today, the Disneyland Resort's second gate, Disney California Adventure, sits across from Disneyland's Main Gate and takes up those extra sixty acres, but in 1955, it was where guests parked their cars. Most people view parking as a pain, but Walt saw it as the start of a story. Ever the showman, Walt pictured his parking lot as the "outer lobby" to the theatre that is Disneyland where costumed parking attendants would act like ushers.

Marquee: Every theatre needs a marquee, and Disneyland is no different. Despite the added cost and risk that no one would climb the stairs to get on board, Walt insisted on elevating his turn-of-the-century-style train station on Main Street. This set an impressive stage and allowed every guest to view the train station from anywhere in the outer lobby, i.e., parking lot.

Inner Lobby: The floral Mickey set below the railroad station at the head of Main Street, USA is one of the most photographed features in the park and a must for virtually every first-time visitor. The next time you are there, or perhaps you have your own photograph and can take a peek now, take a look at the red bricks below the floral. They are a very intentional feature often missed by the average guest. The bricks are red for a reason; they match the red carpet treatment that we readily associate with Hollywood and VIPs. Walt wanted every guest at Disneyland to receive "red carpet" treatment.

Stage Left and Right: Once in the lobby of the floral Mickey, you must make a decision. Will you enter the park via the tunnel on the left or the tunnel on the right? The tunnel entrances further enhance the storytelling stage that is Disneyland. Here you exit the outside world, go "through the screen," and, according to the plaques Walt had hung above the tunnels, enter "the world of Yesterday, Tomorrow, and Fantasy." Be sure to take note of the over-sized "Coming Attractions Posters" that highlight what awaits you in the park. They even pop popcorn in this area as an aromatic reminder of the movie-going experience. For Walt, it was even more than that; he said, "Disneyland is like Alice stepping through the Looking Glass; to step through the portals of Disneyland will be like entering another world."

Opening Scene: Walt wasn't interested in controlling your story. Like any good director, however, he did want to set the opening scene and dictate the opening shot. Main Street, USA might well be the most important area in the park for setting the stage and creating an environment that raises your expectations for a good story. Once you reach the central hub, you have a decision to make. Will you head left into Adventureland or forward into Fantasyland? Choose wisely; all stories hinge on the decisions of their characters and now you're the main character in your Disneyland adventure.

STORY IS KING

HISTORIANS ARE FOND OF DEBATING whether Walt originally set out to be an actor or an animator. Most conclude that he was a frustrated actor but a talented animator. Regardless, the debate is meaningless because it misses the point. At his core, Walt Disney was a storyteller. The question regarding animator versus actor is simply a question of means and method but certainly not one of passion and purpose.

Walt wanted to be remembered as a storyteller. History has been kind to him in that regard. Many on his staff had fond memories of working with Walt, but he is best remembered for being the "best storyteller in the studio." According to *How to Be Like Walt*, Disney animator Dick Huemer recalled that "Walt would take stories and act them out at a meeting, and kill you laughing, they were so funny. You'd have the feeling of the whole thing. You'd know exactly what he wanted."

Walt used story to communicate, connect, and call forth the best in people. An excellent example is when he risked everything to make the world's first full-featured animated film, *Snow White and the Seven Dwarfs*. No one understood *why* Walt wanted to do this. They already had the Mickey Mouse cartoon shorts, along with the associated merchandising, and both were providing the studio and its animators with a steady stream of income during the Great Depression. Once Walt made it clear that he was committed to a full-length animated film, his animators didn't understand *what* he wanted. One evening, feeling frustrated, Walt sent everyone out for dinner on the studio's dime and then called them back for a late night meeting. Ken Anderson, one of the animators who was there that night, according to DisneyInstitute.com, tells us what happened next:

> So we, about forty of us sat there, and we got all settled and Walt was talking to the guys in the front. And he came down the front of the thing and said, 'I'm gonna tell you a story.' He says, 'Been with me all my life.' He said, 'I've lived it.' He started in and told the story of Snow White better than we put it on the screen. He spent from 8:00 to 11:30, and he portrayed all the parts. He had to go forward and back and forward and back and the cutting didn't matter, in order to tell it all and get it all in. But he became even the Queen, he became the Huntsman, he became the dwarves, he became Snow White. And the guy changed. He sat right in front of our eyes and here comes Walt Disney changing. Now there's an enormous talent as an actor;

he could really sell things. And he sold the story to us in such a way that we couldn't believe our ears.

Given Walt's supreme skills as a storyteller, it is no surprise that he constructed Disneyland so story could take center stage. Like every good story, Disneyland is filled with characters, plot, color, detail, and appropriate transitions. As an experienced director, Walt knew what to keep and what to cut. Everything, from the scaled architecture on Main Street to the trashcans in Frontierland, served to support the story. Any incongruities Walt eliminated with ruthless abandon, be it a freeway, which he shielded from his audience by way of the berm, or an unsightly water tower, which he refused to build. Walt may have been the boss of Disneyland, but story was king.

Walt's success can certainly be attributed to his master storyteller abilities. His stories and the stories of Disneyland are lessons we can apply to our own story. The lesson here is two-fold. First, we must make sure we are meeting the needs of those around us by sharing stories. When it came time to share his vision for *Snow White and the Seven Dwarfs* with his team, Walt didn't give them a strategy, statistics, or even a mission statement. Instead, he told a story. In *Business Storytelling for Dummies*, Karen Dietz and Lori L. Silverman write, "When you share a story, you relive an experience and invite others to share in it with you. In this way, you move people from focusing on the tangible and intangible qualities of products and services to memorableness. And today's customers want memorable experiences." Walt understood what people wanted.

Secondly, Walt and Disneyland do not solely remind us of the importance of storytelling. Equally important, both are challenging us to *live* a great story. According to the Disney Family Museum, "Walt wanted guests to feel they had left their own time and journeyed to America at the turn of the twentieth century, ventured into uncharted lands, moseyed through the raucous Wild West, glimpsed the future and stepped into a timeless fantasy world where anything is possible." These stories have meaning, and experiencing these stories can challenge us to make meaningful choices in our own stories, too.

YOU NEED A HERO

ON OPENING DAY, THE BEST stories told by the park were found in Fantasyland, specifically the original "dark rides" of Snow White, Peter Pan, and Mr. Toad. The goal for each was to evoke a specific emotion. Snow White represents drama. Toad serves up humor. Peter Pan provides us with beauty and wonder. Like most of the other attractions, these were crafted at the Disney studio in Burbank and, therefore, constructed by individuals accustomed to building story sets. This began the tradition of Disneyland being home to "attractions" rather than "rides." In his autobiography, Marty Sklar states that before retiring, he reminded those who would succeed him: "When we only describe our attractions as 'rides,' we fall into the category of Six Flags, Knott's, Universal, etc. describing their stuff. We should rise above them (because our stuff does!) and describe what we do as 'attractions, adventures, immersive experiences, and of course stories.'"

The public took immediate notice and loved the difference. Nonetheless, the original Fantasyland dark rides faced a significant challenge, as Sam Gennawey explains in *The Disneyland Story*:

> All the Fantasyland dark rides shared another trait. The guest was supposed to fulfill the role of the lead character. For example, when a guest rode Snow White, they were supposed to be Snow White. The attraction was designed with that point of view in mind. You were the girl that was being threatened...guests were getting confused because they did not see the main character.

It took over twenty-five years, but with the renovation of Fantasyland in 1983, lead characters were finally added to the dark rides to appease the public and assuage the confusion. This did not fix the real-life challenge we all face, however. Too many people live their lives like they are still riding one of these original attractions. We keep looking for the lead character, a hero, not realizing that we are responsible for our own story. I want to encourage you to live a better story by challenging you to take the lead in your life. Be the hero that you, your family, and your business desperately need.

Get busy revising. If you don't like your current story, know that it is never too late to change it. Yes, it will require action and probably conflict.

All good stories do.

And once you take that action, you'll be addicted to the power of story, as author Donald Miller confirms in his book *A Million Miles in a Thousand Years: What I Learned While Editing My Life*: "And once you live a good story, you get a taste for a kind of meaning in life, and you can't go back to being normal; you can't go back to meaningless scenes stitched together by the forgettable thread of wasted time."

"DATA WITH A SOUL"

Speaker and author Brené Brown was the first to reference the power of stories as being "data with a soul." Allow me to share with you a sample of how this statement is true from my current career by comparing statistics vs. story. Knowing my passion for both students and success, my school reached out to me and asked that I develop a program/class to address the needs of students who have historically struggled over the course of multiple semesters. These are individuals with the ability and aptitude for completing college level work. More often than not, the challenges they face reflect a lack of effort rather than a lack of I.Q.

Under this mandate, I and a selected team developed a course on Academic Excellence. Instead of focusing on the traditional academic avenues such as how to take notes, improve study skills, or manage your time better, we focused exclusively on effort. The results?

Statistically, I can tell you thirty-eight students enrolled in ACE, the Academic Course on Excellence, that first fall semester. Twenty-eight passed ACE (because of the effort factor; by definition, if you failed ACE, it is because you didn't really *do* ACE). Out of the twenty-eight who passed, fourteen or 50 percent earned a single semester GPA high enough to continue enrollment—remember, we are working with students serving multiple semesters of probation and suspensions. The average *prior* semester GPA for these fourteen students was 0.9. Not good! However, their average ACE semester GPA stood at an amazing 2.7. Yay!

Those are the numbers. Now allow me to tell you a story. A story I believe puts a face on the numbers and gives the data a soul.

One of the students I mentored in ACE spent several semesters trying to pass her English Capstone Course. This course involved a major writing project of significant length. She was a talented writer, but over time, she had built the project up into a barrier she believed she would never get beyond. The problem wasn't that she was earning an F on the writing; the problem was that she had never actually *done* the writing.

From our first day in ACE, she shared with the group her struggle. Like everyone else, ACE was a form of "GrACE" that represented her last hope. If she ever hoped to graduate, then this semester *had* to be different.

About two-thirds through the term, she came into class distraught. Inconsolable. When I asked her what was wrong, she shared through a cascade of tears that she was repeating herself all over again. The semester was already more than half over, and she was again crapping out on her capstone.

"How much have you written?" I asked.

"None," she confessed to the surprise of no one.

In that moment, I decided to take a chance. I dismissed the rest of the class but asked her to stay behind. Forty-five minutes remained in our class so she still belonged to me. She needed a hero, so I challenged her to step up and take the lead. I instructed her to gather anything she had readily available that would allow her to get to work on writing—emphasizing the effort piece. "You are beating yourself up for failing something you haven't even started."

She spent the next forty-five minutes writing non-stop in our conference room. Her pen never left her paper. When she left for her next class, I asked whether she felt better. "Much," she said, smiling.

The next week, she returned to class a completely different person. She exuded joy and jubilation. Before we even officially started, unable to contain her excitement, she shared with her fellow students that her capstone was complete.

I was stunned. Shocked. "How?" I asked.

She shared with everyone how I had forced her to stay behind the previous week and get started. Once she had started, she wanted to build on that momentum and thus never really wanted to stop. What had historically been an unimaginable impossibility, semester after semester, was now wrapped up and complete—all in one week.

Her final grade? B+!

SOUVENIR STOP

Think in Narrative—Take a moment to write down your greatest current challenge. Instead of being overwhelmed by it or viewing it as an impossibility, think of it in terms of story. What is the plot? Where is the conflict? Who are the characters? What is the ending you truly desire that would make for your best story?

___

___

___

___

___

___

___

"When you think in narrative the world becomes much more interesting and begins to make more sense."

— Mark Levy, *The Accidental Genius*

EDIT YOUR ENDING—A DIRECTOR IS always in charge of the story, and his two most frequent words are "action" and "cut." What action do you need to take to begin living a better story? What do you need to stop doing, i.e., "cut," so you can get what you really want? Remember, you are in the lead. Be your own hero. Provide the plot twist necessary for your unexpected ending.

"Edit your life frequently and ruthlessly. It's your masterpiece after all."

— Nathan W. Morris, author and filmmaker

TELL STORIES—WHEN IS YOUR NEXT presentation? Whom are you trying to persuade? How can you start telling stories so that you, like Walt, can connect and communicate with and call forth the best from those around you?

When I interviewed for my current position, I answered almost every question with a story. As I built my team, I shared story after story, hoping I could connect with each member as quickly as possible. I knew I was on the right track when only a few months in, a team member, Steve, shared that he had to change his running path because he kept seeing coyotes. "I wasn't afraid of the coyotes; I was afraid of your great stories. If anyone ever had a story about a friend who was eaten by a coyote, it would be you. I didn't want to be that friend."

"Great stories happen to those who tell them."

— Author Ira Glass

GETTING YOUR HAND STAMPED

We started this chapter by stating that Disneyland speaks the universal language of story, so it is fitting to conclude it with an international Disneyland story.

Once the Disneyland stage opened and its stories began connecting with the general public, Walt's intended audience, word got out that you didn't want to miss Disneyland. Everyone wanted in on the act, including politicians and international VIPs. Over the years, the Magic Kingdom has played host to hundreds of kings and queens, princes and princesses, presidents, and heads of state. According to *The Disneyland Story*, in the 1970s, a United States State Department official gave the following compliment, "Walt sold America and Americana to foreign dignitaries. I have no doubt that Walt Disney and Disneyland, in a very real way, have contributed to better understanding and a friendlier attitude on the part of world leaders to the U.S."

Famously, however, one international leader did not get his day at Disneyland. In September 1959, at the height of America's Cold War with the Soviet Union, the communist leader Nikita Khrushchev made a visit to the United States and California, and like any average American in 1959, where he wanted to go most was Disneyland. According to Jim Korkis in *The Revised Vault of Walt*, Khrushchev's request, primarily due to security concerns, was refused. Like a petulant child denied his story at bedtime, Khrushchev threw a fit:

> But just now I was told that I could not go to Disneyland. I asked, "Why not?" What is it? Do you have rocket-launching pads there? I do not know. And just listen—just listen to what I was told—to what reason I was told. "We, which means the American authorities, cannot guarantee your security if you go there."
>
> Putting me in a closed car and stewing me in the sun is not the right way to guarantee my safety. This [not being allowed to go

> to Disneyland] development causes me bitter regret. I thought I could come here as a free man.

In his defense, Khrushchev wasn't the only one disappointed. So, too, was Walt. Disneyland had just experienced its first major expansion, in Tomorrowland, and Walt was looking forward to showing off his submarines, "the eighth-largest submarine fleet in the world."

We all need our stories, even despots and dictators. "Other than the total destruction of capitalism and the triumph of communism, what did Khrushchev really want? He wanted to go to Disneyland."

FACING FEAR AND FAILURE

"All the adversity I've had in my life, all my troubles and obstacles have strengthened me.... You may not realize it when it happens, but a kick in the teeth may be the best thing in the world for you."

NOT MY CIRCUS, NOT MY MONKEYS

WITH OVER 650 MILLION VISITORS throughout its history and with replications around the world, Disneyland is an unparalleled success. Six decades later, it is easy to forget that at one point, nearly everyone predicted it would fail. Further, because of its vaunted success, it is also easy to presume that Disneyland has never failed. *This is false.* Like everyone, Disneyland has made its share of mistakes and faced its share of failures.

The first spectacular failure occurred during the first year, 1955, when Walt decided to open the Mickey Mouse Club Circus in November. Walt Disney loved circuses. He remembered them well from when he was a child, even recalling a time when the circus came to town but he could not afford to attend. Undaunted, the young entrepreneur put on his own circus in the family yard and charged his friends for the pleasure of attending his "Greatest Show on Earth." When his mother, Flora, found out what Walt had done, she insisted that he shut it down and return the money.

With Disneyland, Walt now called the shots and could put on whatever show he wished. Main Street, USA was the perfect venue for a traditional circus parade, and the large open space between Fantasyland and Tomorrowland (home to Matterhorn Bobsleds today) was the perfect place to raise the world's largest, striped circus tent. Walt realized his childhood dream by bringing his circus home to Disneyland on November 11, 1955; he even served as the Grand Marshall in his own circus parade. Only this time, he didn't have to worry about refunding anyone's money.

Nobody came.

Okay, *almost* nobody came.

The circus had its own share of challenges, including escaped llamas lumbering down Main Street, animals spitting at guests, and an aerialist trapeze artist soaring through the sky, bare-breasted after losing her not-so-big top. But the true challenge to Disneyland's Mickey Mouse Circus was, well—Disneyland. By 1955, most people had seen a circus, but no one had seen anything quite like the show that is Disneyland. The circus had to compete with too many attractions. As Imagineer Sklar states, "Visitors came to ride Dumbo the Flying Elephant—but not to see elephants in a live circus."

Disappointed, Walt had no choice but to shut down his circus, and the attraction disappeared, after less than a two-month run, on January 8, 1956.

Walt decided to correct his mistake by using the abandoned circus space to create a midget or junior version of the Tomorrowland Autopia. Autopia was one of the most popular, and thus one of the most profitable, opening day attractions. Because crowds were larger than predicted, the park needed as much new ride capacity as possible going into its first, full summer season in 1956, so a second version of Autopia seemed an obvious solution. What also should have been obvious, however, is that creating an additional Autopia that only children could ride violated Walt's vision for creating a park where parents and children could have fun, *together*. Again, Walt quickly realized his mistake and the short version of Autopia had a short-lived time span of only one year.

An old Polish Proverb says, "Not my circus, not my monkeys." It is a reminder to keep away from things you want no part in. Walt's circus failed because people came to Disneyland for other reasons and purposes. They wanted no part of a circus inside "The Happiest Place on Earth."

Likewise, it is natural for you in seeking success to want nothing to do with fear or failure. Fear?

Failure?

Keep me as far away from them as possible. "Not my circus, not my monkeys," right?

But it doesn't work that way. Not only must you face fear and failure, but at some level, you even need to *embrace* fear and failure. Both are strong indicators that you are taking the necessary risks to be successful, and, while it may not seem like it at the time, that you are very much on the right path.

NEVER BEATEN AT ANYTHING

LIKE DISNEYLAND, IT IS ALSO easy to presume that Walt Disney enjoyed a straight and uninterrupted path to success. I open my History of Disneyland class by giving a brief biography of Walt. Today, most people only see Walt through the prism of the parks and films that bear his name, but these are small and distorted windows. My students are shocked to discover that the only thing in Walt's life bigger than his dreams, or the circus tent he once raised in Disneyland, is his long list of failures. Lowlights include:

BANKRUPTCY—THE DISNEY STUDIO IN BURBANK wasn't Walt's first. He started in Kansas City, where he created an often forgotten studio called "Laugh-O-Grams." His distributor cheated him out of money and eventually went bankrupt, forcing Walt to do the same. This failure prompted Walt's fateful move to California in 1923.

Loss of Oswald the Rabbit—As mentioned earlier, Walt's first real success came in the form of Oswald the Lucky Rabbit. Success was short-lived, however, because Walt soon learned that his distributor, Universal, owned the contract rights to the character and was in the process of stealing away the animators who helped bring Oswald to life. After years of struggle and a few brief months of success, Walt was broke again and sitting right back at start.

***Snow White* Sneak Peek**—Before *Snow White and the Seven Dwarfs'* fabled premiere at the Carthay Theatre in downtown Los Angeles on December 21, 1937, Walt first gave a small audience of viewers a "sneak peek" at the world's first, full-length animated film. Walt had everything, including the mortgage on his own home, riding on this picture. Even his own wife, Lilly, and brother, Roy, were against the making of this movie. Walt was horrified when his first audience stood up and walked out halfway through the movie. Little did Walt know that his audience consisted primarily of college students who had to get back before curfew.

***Fantasia* and Other Famous Flops**—Walt's second full-length animated movie, *Fantasia,* never made a profit during Walt's lifetime. *Snow White and the Seven Dwarfs,* the first full-length animated film, was a risky eighty-four minutes long. *Fantasia,* however, runs just over a full two hours. The music alone cost three times the average cost of a Mickey Mouse cartoon and the soundtrack was so elaborate that few theatres were equipped to feature the film. Eventually, even Walt admitted that he had made a mistake in creating it. His other movie that year, *Pinocchio,* also failed to produce a profit during its first box office run. As did *Bambi, Alice in Wonderland,* and despite a castle in

Disneyland providing four years of pre-release promotion, *Sleeping Beauty*.

Flora Disney's Death—The stratospheric success of *Snow White and the Seven Dwarfs* was followed not just with failure (*Fantasia*) but actual tragedy. Using some of the money from *Snow White*, Walt and Roy decided to buy their parents a home in North Hollywood. Elias and Flora moved from Oregon, but Flora quickly complained about the smell of gas in the new home, so Walt sent his studio workers to check out her concerns. They couldn't find anything. A few days later, Walt's mother died of asphyxiation from the furnace's fumes. Inconsolable, Walt blamed himself for his mother's untimely death and rarely, if ever, spoke of the tragedy.

By any measure, Walt Disney lived a successful life; however, it was also filled with failure. Many people avoid success, but it is impossible to avoid fear and failure; they are part of the human experience. If you can't avoid them, then you might as well embrace them, learn from them, and, like Walt, use them to fuel your successes. According to *How to Be Like Walt*, Lillian Disney, Walt's wife, once said, "Walt never thought he was beaten at anything—ever."

Believe in yourself, no matter what. Believe in your ideas, your abilities, your future.

Will you lose sometimes?

Absolutely!

Will you let a loss beat you?

Never!

THE T-REX OF TERROR

At some level, we all have a fear of failure. Fear is a natural part of being human, and failure is a natural part of success. Show me someone who hasn't failed and I will show you someone who simply hasn't bothered to try. You may not realize it, but fear and failure go hand-in-hand.

Early in human history, our fears served us quite well. Fear told our bodies when to flee because a larger or stronger creature was ready to eat us for breakfast. Imagine for a moment that the dinosaurs in the Primeval World attraction (Disneyland Railroad between Tomorrowland and Main Street) were real and the T-Rex suddenly decided you should be his next churro. Fear would fuel your "fight or flight" reflex, and you would, no doubt, flee as quickly as possible. Failure to do so would result in instant death, and for many, death represents the ultimate failure.

In our modern world, we rarely have to deal with the reality of an actual T-Rex profiling us for supper. Sure, there might be a risk we are unwilling to take, a decision we are hesitant to make, or a confrontation we are reluctant to have. As we put these actions off until the proverbial tomorrow, our primal fears from the yesterdays of human history mount. Soon, we become convinced that we have every reason, and more, to feel genuinely afraid. Our inaction paralyzes us, and we become frozen in a primordial soup of procrastination.

Before you get eaten by your own fears, my recommendation is to just STOP.

Take a breath.

Pause.

Isolate what it is that is really paralyzing you. Why are you in such a panic? I am willing to guess, just a hunch here, that whatever it is, it is NOT a Tyrannosaurus Rex. In other words, you might feel afraid (we all do). You might be uncomfortable (it happens). You very well might not know the ultimate outcome of your current situation. (Hello, Adventureland.) But you are going to figure it out, and you will survive it.

In her excellent book, *The Creative Habit,* Twyla Tharp identifies five reasons why people are too afraid to take the risk necessary for living their lives at the next level. In parentheses, I've added why these reasons are all false or illogical:

1. People will laugh at me. (At least you will have a heads up about *why* they are laughing.)
2. Someone has done it before. (We academics are very sensitive to plagiarism.)
3. I have nothing to say. (You do.)
4. I will upset someone I love. (Remember, Walt's own wife and brother didn't believe in his dreams for *Snow White* or Disneyland).
5. Once executed, the idea will never be as good as it is in my mind. (You won't know whether that's true until you execute it.)

Unlike looking for Waldo, I can imagine it wasn't particularly hard for you to find yourself somewhere in the above list. I quickly identified with #1 and #3.

When I set out to teach a college level course on the History of Disneyland, I knew I was pushing the edge of the academic envelope. I feared my colleagues would laugh at my idea.

Even worse, what if they laughed at *me*?

I believed, however, that the story of Disneyland is strong enough, and the history is rich enough, that I could carry the class and connect it to the parallels of United States History from the 1950s and beyond. If I could simply get over my fear of not being able to "sell" the course, I was confident that the actual class would be anything but a failure.

Setting out to write this book has been a completely different story. See #3 above. Sure, the idea of marrying Disneyland and Walt with life lessons and success is a creative concept. But what do I, a U.S. History teacher, really have to say that is of any significance regarding leadership or life? Ironically enough, the night I sat down to write this chapter, I expressed to Niki my fear that I was running out of substantive things to say. I had already penned the most obvious stories and still had two-thirds of a book to write. Then I read Twyla Tharp's words above. Because they mirrored my own fears, they reassured me that I might very well be on the right track.

"Fear is the boss you fight before taking your life to the next level."

— Author Stephen Guise

A ROCKET-SIZED RISK

By the time I visited Disneyland for the first time in August 1988, thirty-three years after its original opening, most of the major bugs and kinks had been well worked out. However, a decade later, I did get to participate in one of the park's more spectacular failures.

In order to keep Tomorrowland about tomorrow, rather than a land that presents the present or even the past, Tomorrowland has gone through more comprehensive overhauls than any other area of the park. The most recent revision took place in 1998. Using a Jules Verne vision of the future, everything was painted bronze, gold, or dark brown, including the iconic white of Space Mountain. The Captain EO attraction was converted over to the more contemporary "Honey, I Shrunk the Audience." The Rocket Jets were relocated to the entrance of Tomorrowland and rebranded as "Astro Orbitor." In addition, a smaller replica of the original TWA Moonliner returned to the land as an homage to the Tomorrowland of opening day.

At the center of the newfangled Tomorrowland was an E-ticket attraction called Rocket Rods. The WEDWay PeopleMover, part of the 1967 Tomorrowland renovation, was removed and replaced by the faster moving Rocket Rods. Despite being a highlight and touted as an E-ticket experience, the attraction lasted a mere three years. (I'll give you the full rundown on what an E-ticket experience is later in the book.)

Enticed by the promise of a "new Tomorrowland" and the expectation of experiencing a new E-ticket attraction, my family made sure to visit in the summer of 1998. During the first two days of our vacation, Rocket Rods was tellingly closed due to technical difficulties—a certain sign of things to come; the ride would eventually be shut down due to insurmountable mechanical challenges. Nonetheless, I wasn't going home without experiencing this new thrill. I made sure we arrived before the park's opening on our final day so I could be one of the first in line when Rocket Rods opened. Sometime around midday, the attraction became available, but by the time I discovered this, the wait was well over three hours. Undeterred, I waited my turn. The main purpose of our trip was to experience the new Tomorrowland, so I wasn't going home without riding the newest, centerpiece thrill.

What a colossal dud!

I've never been a big fan of Autopia, but putzing around at five miles per hour in a car built for small children is far more fascinating than anything offered by Rocket Rods. That one of my all-time favorite attractions, The Peoplemover, was removed to make way for Rocket Rods only makes this memory even more painful.

What is the lesson here? We are all going to fail. Sometimes, our failures might even be of the spectacular, E-ticket variety. If a success like Disneyland doesn't get everything right, chances are you and I won't either.

And that's okay.

I have learned that you cannot protect yourself from fear. In fact, when you protect yourself from fear, the only thing you succeed in doing is protecting yourself from success.

"Fear isn't only a guide to keep us safe; it's also a manipulative emotion that can trick us into living a boring life...the great stories go to those who don't give in to fear."

— Donald Miller

DRAWING ON FAILURE

Tim Brown of the Stanford Design group does an interesting experiment with his students. He gives them a pencil, a blank piece of paper, and thirty seconds. The challenge is to draw your neighbor and then share your picture with him or her. (Learn more at https://www.ted.com/speakers/tim_brown.)

Imagine for a moment that you were in a class and given the above task. Rarely, if ever, does the Walt Disney in any of us rise to the rescue. Instead, adults hate this exercise—with a fiery passion. During the course of the expiring thirty seconds, it is not at all uncommon to hear words such as "This is horrible," "I'm sorry," or "I've never been so embarrassed." And this is just during the drawing stage. When it comes time to share the pictures, the pleas for mercy become deafening.

Now imagine for a moment that you were to try this experiment with a classroom of children. Can you remember the undiscovered, unlimited wonderment of being a kid? All youngsters fancy themselves to be Picasso incarnate. Every drawing is a masterpiece. Every doodle deserves valuable real estate in the only art gallery that ever really matters, the family refrigerator.

Something sad happens on the road to responsibility.

As we transition from childhood into adulthood, our inner critic takes over and we become terrified of our own ideas. We stifle our creativity. We stop drawing. Stop daring. Stop dreaming. It is far better that we censor ourselves than we risk judgment and expose ourselves to the ridicule of our peers.

Let's imagine for just a moment that Walt shared the same mentality. In the face of fear, failure, and the scorn of his inner critic, what would have happened to the idea of Disneyland, birthed on a park bench, if he had successfully censored himself?

Nothing.

For many of us, our lives and our worlds would be so much less without Walt's dreams and his willingness to embrace fear and failure to see those dreams to fruition.

What's holding you back?

It is time for you to step up. It is time for you to show up. We need you.

"The tragedy of life is often not in our failure,
but rather in our complacency; not in our doing too much,
but rather in our doing too little; not in our living above our
ability, but rather in our living below our capacities."

— Benjamin E. Mays

SOUVENIR STOP

When Disneyland first opened, Walt had no choice but to cede control of the retail operations within the park. He could barely afford to build the attractions, so he certainly didn't have the extra funds necessary for stocking stores. Nor did Walt have the know-how necessary to make these enterprises possible. Instead, he focused on learning how to run the park and leased out the retail space, especially on Main Street, U.S.A., to outside vendors. With the success of the park, Walt was in a much better position to take over these operations when the original leases ran out, typically five years after opening.

As an homage to those first five years, I am ceding control to the Souvenir Stop for this chapter. I want to introduce you to Jonathan Fields. Jonathan is a New York City dad, husband, and lawyer turned award-winning author, media-producer, and entrepreneur. His last book, *Uncertainty: Turning Fear and Doubt into Fuel for Brilliance* was named the top personal development book in 2011 by 800-CEO-READ. His piece "Life is a Contact Sport," posted at his website www.jonathanfields.com is the best possible takeaway for this chapter.

Enjoy.

Life Is a Contact Sport

There's only so much you can learn about yourself by thinking:

Am I good enough?

Are my ideas good enough?

Am I ready to go public, speak, launch, write?

Who's really going to listen to me?

What if I fail? What if I succeed?

What if my assumptions are massively wrong, or right?

You can spin these questions in your head ad nauseam. Most people do.

But, you know what's happening while you're lost in the process of arguing both sides of every conversation ever had in your head?

Life.

Life is happening. But not yours.

Your life is on hold. Being kept from happening by the merciless cacophony of conversation that spirals and splinters through your brain, leaving you incapable of action. Paralyzed.

Among my close friends, colleagues and those I've been blessed to work with, I've gotten a bit of a reputation for being, how do I say this…kind, but blunt. I try to be gentle, but I don't sugarcoat. One of the things I've ended up saying over and over is…

Get out of your head and into the world.

A bit of introspection, contemplation and internally-birthed wisdom is good. But all too often, we try to find answers in the world inside us that exist only through engaging with the world around us. We choose guessing over testing, because we're terrified of failing, or being wrong and then being judged.

Here's the deal.

You will be wrong. You will be judged.

You will be awful as often as you are awesome. People will know when you mess up.

Will that hurt? Depends.

If your ego and your metric for success are tied to being right, then yes. It'll suck.

If your ego and your metric for success are tied to action and learning, then the suck-factor becomes overpowered by the fact that, in moving an idea from that cerebral pit of despair known as your mind, and putting it into the world to generate information, data, knowledge, you've already won. And the data that comes from your "test," whether it validates or obliterates your assumptions, lays the foundation for growth.

Only when you get out of your head do you create the opportunity to know, not guess, if you are good enough, if "it" is good enough. If you are, how wonderful. And, if you're not, how wonderful that you now know, and you can stop frittering away your life with merciless self-talk…and DO something about it.

Simple fact…

Life is a contact sport.

It's about engaging with, rather than hiding from the world. You can't avoid the contact, without also avoiding the life. Does that mean you run recklessly into it?

Some people do. It's the running with scissors or running with the bulls approach. Too much machismo and risk for me. And likely for you.

I tend to take a more "artisanal" approach to engaging my ideas with life. I start in my head, let the concepts gestate, but not for too long. Then I choose a palate or channel or medium or outlet to begin to test elements of my ideas and my own personal capabilities.

Example? I test concepts for books and articles, for media and art, for future merchandise and shows on social media all the time. I do calls or impromptu meetings, gatherings or workshops to both offer value, but simultaneously test snippets.

Standup comedians are legendary for this. They'll workshop an act for months or even years to get a single set nailed down. Seinfeld is famous for working a single line for years to refine it. And I've no doubt, his joke graveyard exponentially outsizes his list of epic snort-laughs.

We're like those comics, doesn't matter how funny the line is in your head, if the audience hates it, it's gotta go. All the contemplation and introspection in the world will not tell you how it's going to land. Only one way to get your answer.

Get out of your head and into the world. So, here's my invitation...

You know that thing you've been arguing both sides of in your head?

C'mon. You know. If you don't, I can virtually guarantee you're lying to yourself.

Stop. Now.

Ask yourself...

> *What single action can I take today that will replace my assumptions with information?*

Then take that action.

Engage. Contact. Live.

GETTING YOUR HAND STAMPED

Disneyland opened as the "house for the mouse." Over time, Mickey was joined by a whole cast of characters, including princes, princesses, villains, and even Pixar characters. If Disney drew the character, then you can find it, at home, in Disneyland.

Except one.

For over eighty years, Oswald the Rabbit was nowhere to be found in the Disney universe. Fans clamored for him, but he was hopelessly lost to Universal. His cartoons no longer ran after 1943, but his rights remained in the wrong hands. Seemingly, nothing could be done to bring Oswald back.

But time heals all wounds, even those inflicted in the face of fear and failure and absorbed by an anthropomorphic animated character. In 2006, NBC television, owned by Universal, won the valuable NFL rights to newly created *Sunday Night Football*. They wanted a star announcer to carry the broadcast and coveted Al Michaels, who was still under contract with ABC.

So they made a trade instead.

Just as NBC was owned by Universal, ABC was now owned by Disney. Disney was willing to release Al if, and only if, Universal was finally willing to return the rights to long-lost Oswald, and all of the original Oswald cartoons created by Walt, back over to Disney.

And so, after eighty long years and a rather unusual trade, Oswald the Lucky Rabbit finally came home, to Disneyland.

But unlike Walt's circus, Oswald is home to stay.

MASTERING THE 4 Cs

"Somehow I can't believe there are any heights that can't be scaled by a man who knows the secret of making dreams come true. This special secret, it seems to me, can be summarized in four Cs: Curiosity, Confidence, Courage and Constancy and the greatest of these is confidence."

THE BROADWAY MUSICAL *SMILE* HAS a song titled "I Want to Live in Disneyland." The song is about how everything would be okay if only we could live in Disneyland. I first heard this song while walking through downtown Riverside during Christmas break several years ago. At first, I only heard the word "Disneyland." Naturally, any mention of Disneyland mesmerized me immediately, so I sauntered over to hear the remainder of the lyrics. The song echoes what I have thought and felt for many, many years:

I want to live in Disneyland.

I want to make my home in Disneyland. Why can't I live in Disneyland?

Instead, I live in the world of Higher Education where the frequent refrain among students is "Cs Get Degrees." The melody of mediocrity. As leaders, we, of course, are aiming for a significantly higher standard. Walt Disney, in his infinite wisdom, sets this standard with his chorus of the 4 Cs: Curiosity, Confidence, Courage, and Constancy. Let's talk about each one of these.

CURIOSITY

A CURIOUS CORPORATE VALUE

Walt transformed his personal curiosity into a corporate value. He used it to propel his team members forward with new visions and new challenges. He was always interested in what was around the corner, be it sound in animation ("Steamboat Willie"), the making of the first full-length animated feature (*Snow White and the Seven Dwarfs*), or building his first theme park (Disneyland). Along the way, people who knew more tried to tell Walt "No." Walt, however, almost always knew better. Over time, his employees learned not to tell Walt "No." Walt was just curious enough to keep pushing his people until they could finally find the "Yes" he had been looking for all along. According to *How to Be Like Walt,* "Walt had this great curiosity. He was very excited about what he was doing. He lived and breathed it, and finally it rubbed off on you."

IN THE TIKI, TIKI, TIKI, TIKI, TIKI ROOM

In 1963, Walt took his curiosity and combined it with his advancements in sound, show, and theme park technology to create an entirely new form of animation, audio-animatronics. Just as Walt revolutionized animation by giving life to cartoon characters, he now wanted to do the same with three-dimensional figures.

A few years earlier, while on vacation in his favorite American city, New Orleans, Walt came across an antique mechanical singing bird. Curious about how it worked, he purchased the treasure and brought it home. But instead of placing it in a curio cabinet and forgetting about it, he instructed his Imagineers to take it apart and figure out how it worked.

This curiosity led to the world's first audio-animatronic attraction, Walt Disney's Enchanted Tiki Room, which opened in Disneyland on June 23, 1963. Originally envisioned as a dinner show with the birds singing only at the end, the attraction morphed into a seventeen-minute serenade of 225 birds, tiki gods, and flowers. The combination of sound, electronics, and animation was so mesmerizing that the "barker bird," Juan, working solo (he was, after all, the only "Juan") at the attraction's entrance caused crowds to stop as they were entering or exiting Adventureland. This was hot stuff for the early 1960s, so hot that the Tiki Room became Disneyland's first air-conditioned attraction; the air-conditioning was necessitated by all of the giant computers and electronics stored underneath the floor.

I first experienced Walt Disney's Enchanted Tiki Room in 1974. This was the replica in Florida, however, rather than the original in California. Nonetheless, the shows are essentially the same. My dad, mom, and all four kids waited nearly three hours on a warm, muggy August evening to experience what today takes no more than twenty minutes—the amount of time it takes for a single show to cycle through. A colleague, Dr. Tim Brady, who holds a Doctorate in Computer Education, once explained to me how technology is always relative by defining it as "anything invented or created after you were born." In 1974, the audio-animatronics aviary that is the Tiki Room was still space-age stuff, so we were all curious to see it.

Just as the doors were opening and we were walking in, my youngest sister, then three and barely out of diapers, announced that she needed to go to the bathroom.

"Now?" my mom asked.

"Yes!" she replied. "It's an emergency!"

Panicked, my parents assessed the situation and made a daring decision. There was no way they were going to get out of line and endure another three-hour wait. Knowing that being potty trained was a rather recent development for my sister, they told her just to go in her pants. They would simply deal with the aftermath sometime after the show.

Being a boy, and all of ten at the time, I never forgot that scene or the show. Sitting there that evening, I improvised my own version of the famous Sherman Brothers song that accompanies the attraction.

All together now:

"In the PeePee, PeePee, PeePee, PeePee, PeePee Room! In the PeePee, PeePee, PeePee, PeePee, PeePee Room!"

Today, audio-animatronics are synonymous with the Disney theme park experience. The technology of this art has evolved over time and is best seen in Disneyland's Pirates of the Caribbean, the last attraction Walt worked on before his death in December, 1966. It all started years earlier, however, with Walt's childlike curiosity.

CURIOUS, LIKE A KID

CAN YOU REMEMBER WHAT IT was like to be a kid? Children need to know things. No question goes unasked. Kids never leave a rock unturned. For children, the curiosity of life knows no limits. Every day, they wake up exploring the world and seeking to know more about everything around them.

Somewhere on the road from being a kid to being an adult, too many of us stop being curious. Perhaps we think we already know it all? Maybe you believe that your experiences and your worldview are all you need to know? Did you get criticized once for asking a "stupid" question, so you have been careful with questions ever since? Regardless of the reason, I want to give you permission, right now, to get curious again. Curiosity is how we learn. Walt understood that, as Williams and Denney illustrate in *How to Be Like Walt*:

> Walt had a childlike way about him.... A four-year old will stop and look at a blade of grass and think it's the greatest thing he's ever seen. Most adults lose that natural curiosity, but not Walt. He was always seeing possibilities and wonder in the simplest things. He never lost his childlike curiosity about life.

The key to curiosity is staying open and childlike. We need to keep ourselves open to new ideas. Open to new experiences. Open to new adventures.

"We keep moving forward, opening new doors, and doing new things, because we are curious—and curiosity keeps leading us down new paths."

— Walt Disney

CONFIDENCE

A WELLSPRING OF CONFIDENCE

IN DISNEYLAND'S EARLY YEARS, ITS most child-friendly place wasn't found in Fantasyland. Instead, that distinction belonged to Frontierland, the Rivers of America, and specifically, Tom Sawyer Island. The ideas for this area are a tribute to Walt Disney's childlike curiosity and imagination. The execution of these ideas are a byproduct of Walt's extreme confidence.

First, creating a permanent riverbed in the parched orange groves of Southern California proved problematic. After dredging the river, engineers went to fill the Rivers of America and were aghast as they watched the sun-soaked soil absorb every drop. They explored multiple solutions, but none worked. Walt, ever-confident in his dream and his team, told them to, "Keep trying—you'll find something." Sure enough, they did.

Secondly, the water flowed even *after* Walt refused to take the time and expense to build pumps. Engineers argued that the pumps were necessary to move the water from the low point of the wells to the higher plane where the Rivers of America sat. "No, just cut a flume to the river and turn the water on," Walt insisted. Finally, they did as instructed and the water flowed just as Walt, with a well of confidence, had predicted. Unbeknownst to all, Walt had taken the time to visit with the landowners the year before; he had curiously quizzed them on all kinds of matters, including the orange groves' irrigation. The surveyors' maps were wrong, but Walt was right.

Lastly, the island that sits in the middle of the river was an item of intense debate and speculation. Prospective plans included scale-model reproductions of famous American buildings, e.g., Mount Vernon and Monticello and/or replications of American river towns such as New Orleans. Ultimately, Walt paid attention to his audience, the public, and responded accordingly. In *The Disneyland Story*, Sam Gennawey observes, "Walt saw a different need. He knew that children needed an opportunity to run free and play, to use their own imaginations, and to create their own personal stories. With the island, he had the opportunity to combine control with the chaos."

Today, Tom Sawyer Island stands as the only attraction anywhere in the world singlehandedly designed by Walt Disney. Other Imagineers were assigned the project, but none could do it to Walt's liking. Frustrated, Walt worked throughout the evening one night and then laid the plan on an Imagineer's desk the next morning. He told his team, with confidence, "Now *that's* the way it should be."

THE GREATEST OF THESE

As we can see from Walt's quote at the beginning of this chapter, he did not consider all of the 4 Cs to be created equal. When the Apostle Paul writes on Faith, Hope, and Love in the New Testament, he quickly identifies Love as being "the greatest of these." Similarly, Walt singles out confidence as the greatest of the 4 Cs. Like children who want to spend all day on Tom Sawyer Island, or people like me who want to live in Disneyland, we need to camp here for a bit to appreciate fully Walt's wisdom.

When I initially outlined the chapters for this book, I toyed with the idea of only writing a chapter about "Facing Failure" rather than

"Facing *Fear* and Failure." I knew that this chapter on Mastering the 4 Cs would include sections on both courage and confidence. Combined, I assumed that we could face fear collectively by covering failure, courage, and confidence. Of course, we now know that fear and failure are inextricably linked to success. In similar fashion, failure is also linked to confidence. Allow me to explain.

For far too long, I bought into the popular, Pollyanna-notion that confidence is simply a construct of positive thinking. Just believe that good things will happen and they will. Trust that everything will turn out okay and it inevitably does.

I think I can. I think I can. I think I can. But what if you can't?

What if it doesn't? What happens then?

Plant yourself on this planet long enough and you will soon learn that bad things happen. Sometimes, very bad things happen. I like to think of myself as a "glass is half-full" kind of guy. But I now know that confidence goes deeper than what you believe about water sitting in a glass.

Much deeper.

Walt Disney was aware of this as well. "I always look on the optimistic side of life, but I am realistic enough to know that life is a complex matter." Further, when it came to exposing children to the realities of our world and conflict in his animated stories, he shared that "life is composed of lights and shadows and we would be untruthful, insincere, and saccharine if we tried to pretend there were no shadows."

In other words, confidence isn't about tricking yourself by way of positive thinking into believing there are no shadows. Rather, confidence is knowing *beyond a shadow of a doubt* that regardless of how your risk turns out, you will, in fact, *be okay!*

DEAN OF NOT SUPPOSED TO BE HERE

Despite my extended career in higher education, I didn't get into college the conventional way. I never submitted an admissions application, nor did I ever take an ACT or SAT exam.

Why?

First, I didn't even know I wanted to go to college until halfway through my senior year of high school. I picked a school in Mississippi, a four-hour drive from my home in the Florida Panhandle, based on the recommendation of a friend and the availability of the major I was interested in pursuing.

I went for a preview weekend that spring and walked away having learned my first lesson: college is expensive! No one in my family had ever gone to college so there were no preparations, financial or otherwise, for me to attend school beyond free, public education. If I wanted to pursue higher education, no one was going to stop me.

But I didn't have any support, either. I was on my own.

I decided to stay home my first year after high school. My plan was to work, save, and then go to college a year later. Instead, I worked, spent, and found myself even more broke than I was at my high school graduation. At least then I had cards and cash celebrating my achievement. But that money was now long gone, most of it destined for my arcade addiction and my ongoing affair with Ms. Pac-Man.

I received a phone call one morning from a friend, Don, who had originally recommended the school in southern Mississippi. He asked whether I was still interested in attending. When I told him yes, he said that he had his affairs in order and was leaving the next day. Was I interested in joining him? I checked my social calendar (empty) and readily agreed. As I began packing up my room, my mom walked by and asked why all of my stuff was suddenly in boxes. I told her that Don was heading off to college and I was going to go with him. "That's nice," she replied. The next morning, she handed me a twenty-dollar bill, kissed my forehead, and encouraged me to "Have a nice life."

When Don and I arrived at school, I realized I had more challenges than just money. Apparently, colleges expect you to apply and announce some sort of intention of actually attending before you just show up in the Admissions office at the start of a new semester. I entered the main administration building and took my place in the back of a long line that wasn't heading into Space Mountain. Instead, students who had actually done their homework ahead of time were picking up their admission packets, room assignments, orientation schedules, etc. I simply stood back and observed. A regular routine was in play that I was able to pick up on quickly. When it was my turn, I simply repeated what I had seen all of the students before me do. I gave the student worker my name and she disappeared into a back room to find my admission packet. Typically, this only took a few seconds. In my case, however, because *there was no packet,* I had to wait a few minutes.

Finally, the student worker returned, exasperated, and told me that she had looked everywhere but couldn't find anything on me. I told her there was no need for an apology, and that I would be happy to fill everything out there. She apologized again and asked me whether I minded. Nope! She then told me she didn't know whether they had a place for me to stay in the dormitory because somehow all of my paperwork had been lost. Again, I told her no worries because I had a friend from high school I could stay with. Relieved, she smiled and thanked me for being so cooperative.

The next day was registration day. In 1982, computers were such a rarity that registration took place manually. Tables were set up in the cafeteria and there were piles and piles of legal pads strewn across the formica. Each pad represented a class, and if you wanted to register for one, you simply put your name on the respective pad. I had not met with an advisor, so I just went from table to table and registered my name in every class that sounded interesting. Twenty-one units is a bit much for a first-time, full-time freshman. But at nineteen, you don't know what you don't know.

Exiting the cafeteria and concluding the registration process required one final, interminable line where everything was tallied and you reconciled your registration with your finances. Apparently, this process was serious stuff because the actual vice president of finance was personally sitting at the end of the line and making sure everything was copacetic for each exiting student. My tuition total, including room, board, and books came to $3,862. I looked the vice president of finance in the eye and told him I didn't *quite* have $3,862. He asked me what I did have? I told him I had twenty dollars that I would be happy to split with him. He took the ten bucks and I never looked back.

Obviously, I didn't go to college on ten dollars alone. It took a ton of financial aid, student loans, and working throughout the course of my college career before I could graduate.

But that isn't the point.

The point is that I had enough confidence in myself to show up, get admitted, and pass through the registration line on guile and ten dollars. What did I have to lose?

If I had failed, what was the worst that could have happened? The school could have always sent me back home, which is exactly where I would have been even without ever trying.

Again, confidence isn't knowing that you will succeed. Confidence is knowing that you will be okay *even* when you fail.

And you *will* fail.

COURAGE

ALWAYS TELL THE TRUTH

Because of his original vision for Disneyland, building a place where parents and children could have fun together, Walt was reluctant to have thrill rides in his Magic Kingdom. The Casey Jr. Circus Train in Fantasyland was Walt's version of a Disneyland roller coaster. It opened two weeks after opening day; however, delayed due to challenges during testing, Imagineers were forced to scale back even further its already mild-mannered thrills.

This "no thrills" mindset began to change with the addition of the Matterhorn Bobsleds, which required building the first of Disney's many mountains, in 1959. The pace of adding thrill attractions accelerated after Walt's death in 1966. This change was necessitated by local and national competition in the theme park business, a business virtually started by Walt. In order to continue capturing the imaginations of new generations, the park has no choice but to evolve and incorporate attractions of all kinds, including roller coasters, water flumes, and space simulators.

Today, it is fun to watch families divided over who is going to ride what and with whom. There are always the young, brave souls who, assuming they meet the minimum-height requirement, are willing to try anything. In addition, there are also the old souls who, regardless of age, find the feckless flumes on Pirates of the Caribbean too much to take.

I believe the ride that provides the greatest thrill is actually inside Disneyland's "second gate," aka Disney California Adventure (opened in the old Disneyland parking lot in February 2001). This park houses a number of thrills, including a boardwalk-style Ferris wheel and a roller coaster with an inverted loop, which were originally received by the public as "anti-Disneyland."

In 2004, the Hollywood Tower of Terror opened. At 199 feet, the structure towers above the entire resort, both California Adventure and Disneyland. This immense, themed attraction takes riders up elevator shafts and then takes them through six, *count them*, six randomly computer-generated drop sequences. It is a unique experience that is loved by many, and hated by many more.

The first time I ever rode the Hollywood Tower of Terror was on my and Niki's honeymoon in August, 2009. It had been eight years since my last visit, and it was the newest E-ticket attraction that I couldn't wait to experience.

Niki, however, wasn't so sure.

While standing in line and taking in the impressively immersive queue, we came across another couple also riding for the first time. The young girl was out of her mind with terror. She wanted nothing to do with the ride and had only agreed to ride because her boyfriend wanted to go so badly. I tried to reassure her by telling her that the attraction's line was far scarier than the actual ride.

"All they are going to do is take you up, open a window, give you a gorgeous view of the park from high above, and then they will bring you down."

Always tell the truth.

Just don't *always* be telling it.

"Really?" she responded. "I should be able to handle that."

I looked over at the boyfriend and gave him a knowing nod. The elevator opened up and, like cattle on their way to slaughter, we were loaded into our shaft. With our seatbelts locked, the final cast member spiel spoken, and the doors closed, I looked over at the young lady and declared, "You are so screwed."

If it makes you feel better, years later I still wake up to the sounds of the girl's screams echoing through the night. I revel in the memory, smile, roll over, and return to my slumber.

I always tell the truth. Sometimes, it's even fun.

A BOTTOMLESS PIT OF COURAGE

You have to make the conscious choice to be courageous. What you desire most exists just beyond your comfort zone. You can stay comfortable by avoiding the risks and sitting it out on the sidelines. When you make that choice, however, you are not only avoiding the risks, but you are also denying yourself the thrill of success.

Throughout his life, Walt made the conscious and courageous choice. After going bankrupt in Kansas City, he packed a single suitcase and moved across the country, to California, with forty dollars in his pocket. The only thing he had less of than money was the promise of success. Despite that, Walt believed in his dream and was brave enough to follow it.

In the 1930s, the easier and safer choice would have been to continue to make cartoon shorts and rely on the Mickey Mouse merchandising money. Walt wanted to push the boundaries of animation, however, and thus, he risked it all again to make *Snow White and the Seven Dwarfs*. A summary of quotes from both Walt and Roy, taken from the Disney Family Museum, puts their brave courage into perspective:

> **Walt:** But we had decided there was only one way we could successfully do *Snow White*, and that was to go for broke, shoot the works. There would be no compromise on money, talent or time. We did not know whether the public would go for a cartoon feature, but we were darned sure that audiences wouldn't buy a *bad* cartoon feature. As the *Snow White* budget climbed, I did begin to wonder whether we would ever get our investment back.
>
> **Roy:** There was a period of great tension because, for us, a million and a half dollars was a terrific investment. We had been spending thirty thousand dollars on a cartoon short, but it was guaranteed to us, practically, by our distributor. We got that when we delivered the picture. But if we had flopped with *Snow White*, we were gonna flop with our own money.
>
> **Walt:** I had always objected to letting any outsider see an incomplete motion picture, but I had to sit alone with Joe Rosenberg of the Bank of America and try to sell him a quarter of a million dollars' worth of faith. He showed not the slightest reaction to what he viewed. After the lights came on he walked out of the projection room, remarked that it was a nice day—and yawned! He was still deadpan as I conducted him to his car. Then he turned to me and said, 'Walt, that picture will make a potful of money.' To this day, he's my favorite banker.

Of course, it is one thing to risk nothing when you have nothing, such as when Walt moved to California in 1923. It is a different story, however, when you risk everything when you have everything, which is exactly what Walt did with Disneyland in 1955. He mortgaged everything, including his reputation, to build what everyone else simply said could not be done. But it was in the face of criticism that Walt was often most courageous. As Pat Williams and Jim Denney express in *How to Be Like Walt*, "Psychological studies show that high achieving, successful people are not overly concerned about what others think. This was true of Walt Disney. He never catered to his critics. He never worried about rejection. He kept selling his dreams."

One of the original features on Tom Sawyer Island was Injun Joe's Cave. I can remember going out to Disney World's version when I was ten and needing all the courage I could muster to finish the tour. Inside the cave was a "bottomless pit." I couldn't imagine such a thing and vividly remember being frightened by the prospect of such a pit. What exactly does "bottomless" mean? And how do you find out? I didn't really want to know, so I didn't dare get anywhere near it.

I now know, of course, that there is no such thing. In fact, the bottomless pit in Injun Joe's Cave was never more than seven feet deep. Granted, still a bit over my head in my grown up state of 5' 7¾", but nothing that ever called for true courage.

You need to know, going in, however, that aside from a wellspring of confidence, following your dreams will also require a bottomless pit of courage. However hard you think it will be, it will be harder. However long you think it will take, it will take longer. However much you think it will cost, it will cost twice as much.

But don't you dare sit it out. Don't you dare stop.

Don't you ever give up.

The next time the odds are stacked against you and you don't have the courage to keep moving forward, remember Walt. Do you have more at risk than he did?

I didn't think so.

No one is ever going to believe in you, and your dream, more than you.

Be brave and courageous.

Most importantly, keep moving forward.

"Walt lived the life of his own imagination. Most people are afraid to do that, but Walt was fearless that way."

— *How to Be Like Walt*

CONSTANCY

EXCELLENCE IS A HABIT

I FELL IN LOVE WITH Disney Parks on my first trip to Disney World in 1974. Eighteen years later, I would begin my love affair with Disneyland. I did not become fully immersed, however, until after moving to Southern California in 2011. Since then, Niki and I have visited Disneyland well over 150 times...and counting.

One might wonder whether visiting that frequently takes away the magic, the mystery? Actually, the opposite is true. Yes, we experience the park differently than we did on our first visit or even our tenth. But the magic and the mystery still remain. In fact, having the opportunity to visit that frequently has only managed to impress us even more.

For example, it mystifies me how a place as special as Disneyland can possibly remain so consistently special and magical. I have been to Disneyland throughout every month of the year. I have been to Disneyland on the hottest of summer days and the coldest of winter nights. I have been there in the midst of a driving rainstorm, and I have been there at the end of the rainless summers. I have been there when the crowds were bulimically thin, and I have been when there were more people than pilgrims at Mecca. In other words, I have experienced Disneyland through and through.

Disneyland sets in concrete what Aristotle once said, "We are what we repeatedly do. Excellence, then, is not an act, but a habit." I am in the habit of going to Disneyland because Disneyland is in the habit of being excellent. The repeated excellence of Disneyland motivates and inspires me. Before 1985, Disneyland was closed on Mondays and

Tuesdays throughout most of the year. Partly, this was due to attendance patterns and partly to address routine maintenance needs. Today, the park is open 365 days a year.

I find this inspiring because too many of us, myself included, only want to be excellent when we feel like being excellent. Know, however, that what you do on each and every day counts far more than when you and your excellence only show up every now and then. The people at Disneyland "turn the park over" day in and day out, 365 days per year. Disneyland *always* shows up. As leaders, we need to be sure we are doing the same.

SHOWING UP EVERY DAY

IN THE LATE 1990s, NBC news anchor Tom Brokaw wrote the best-selling book *The Greatest Generation*. This book chronicles the stories of World War II veterans who, by the end of the twentieth century, were dying at the rate of 1,000 per day. Tom believed this generation had remained mostly silent regarding their sacrifices in both the Depression of the 1930s and the ensuing worldwide conflicts of the 1940s. As a journalist, Tom wanted to tell the stories of this particular generation before they had passed and it was too late.

As a history professor with a passionate interest in the events of World War II, I was captivated by the book. I was particularly enamored with how Tom took the generalized story of World War II, which I already knew well, and personalized it. This perspective permitted me to see that the privileges we enjoy today are a consequence of the service and sacrifice of those who have gone before.

When I read about the various hardships and suffering endured by this so-called "Greatest Generation," I was struck by the realization that I am a member of what one day might be remembered, at best, as the "Lamest Generation." When it comes to personal sacrifice, service, or hardship, I am only ever first in line to lodge my own litany of whines, moans, and complaints.

Because of the book's impact and influence, I reflected on areas in my life that I wanted to improve. Consistent exercising immediately came to mind. I was living the life that Benjamin Franklin once warned about, "He that is good at making excuses is seldom good for anything else." I then made the conscious choice (success is *always* a choice) that I was going to spend 1999 walking a minimum of four miles every single day. I knew that, regardless of conditions, I wasn't going to be facing anything close to what members of Brokaw's "Greatest Generation" had faced during their season of suffering and sacrifice.

On December 31, 1999, the last day of the twentieth century, I accomplished my daily goal. Fifteen years later, walking a minimum of four miles every day during a single calendar year remains one of my proudest achievements. Again, success is a choice, and one of the best choices we can make is being consistent whenever possible.

SOUVENIR STOP

The Emporium on Main Street is Disneyland's largest store. "Mastering the 4 Cs" is our longest chapter, so consider this Souvenir Stop your journey through the Main Street Emporium. We have a bit of browsing to do here.

Create a Curio Cabinet—We all have questions, curiosities, reading, and research we would like to do. How are you on your follow through?

Below, I want you to write down three questions you have about your dream, your goal, and your success. Once you write these down, commit to following up on your questions in the next seven days. Take what you learn and allow it to create a path that leads you to even greater discoveries.

____

____

____

As a bonus, find someone whose success looks like something you would like to achieve. Ask him (or her) out to lunch and invite him to share his story by asking questions about how he arrived where he is. Leaders and successful people are rarely shy about sharing their journey with others; most will be honored that you have asked. Use this to your advantage by getting curious.

"I have no special talents,
I am only passionately curious."

— Albert Einstein

PUTTING THE "CON" IN "CONFIDENCE"—MOST people believe that confidence naturally follows success. It is actually the exact opposite. Success might bring you *more* confidence, but you must begin with confidence if you ever hope to see success.

One of the best strategies for gaining the confidence you need is to start "acting as if." Don't wait around to begin behaving like a leader or dressing like a success. Take action now by "acting as if" what you desire most already exists. Examples include:

1. If you want to be happy, then act happier.
2. If you want to be energetic, then act energetically.
3. If you want to be a writer, then start writing and tell people you are a writer.
4. If you want to lose weight, then go buy one outfit that will fit you perfectly at your desired weight. Make your purchase with confidence, *knowing* you *will* achieve your goal.

Use the lines below and commit to taking three "act as if" actions over the next thirty days. Whatever your dream might be, don't worry about not knowing if you can achieve it. "Act as if" anyway and just see what follows. You might not know that you "can," but you don't know that you "can't," either.

1. ____

____

2. ____

____

3. ____

____

Also pay attention to the way you talk to yourself, and others, about your dreams, goals, and successes. No one will ever have more confidence in your dream than you. Use the space below to write three affirmations about yourself and your dream. What you say speaks volumes about your confidence and will go a long way toward the actions you do or don't take.

1. ____

____

2. ____

____

3. ____

____

"We believed in our idea, a family park where parents and children could have fun, together."

— Walt Disney

FORTUNE FAVORS THE BOLD—HISTORY IS written by the people who take action, not those who skip the ride due to fear. What is your history? What do you want your story to be?

Success doesn't happen by chance. You are going to have to take bold, brave steps toward change. Humans are naturally uncomfortable with change and your discomfort calls for courage.

Think about your dream and an uncomfortable step you know you need to take. Write this action down and then find a "battle buddy," a friend or family member, who will hold you accountable for taking action regardless.

Action: ____

____

"All of our dreams can come true,
if we have the courage to pursue them."

— Walt Disney

Create a Mini-Habit—You have a long journey ahead. It is tempting to believe that willpower and motivation will see you through to the end. *They won't.* You need to put in place habits that become second nature to the success you are pursuing.

Author Stephen Guise writes extensively about the practice of "mini-habits." His idea is that we can re-wire our brains toward success by acting consistently using mini-actions, behaviors, and habits on a daily basis that are so small that it is impossible to fail at them. Of course, you can always do more, and you often will, but a mini-habit represents your minimum requirement for each and every day. Examples include:

1. Writing fifty words per day
2. Doing one push-up each day
3. Walking one mile each day
4. Doing five minutes of meditation each day
5. Asking one question each day
6. Working five minutes on your dream each day

The examples are endless, but I think you get the idea. What mini-habit are you willing to commit to doing daily? Write it down in the space below and then take the time to get started. Start today, not tomorrow.

____

____

____

____

For what it's worth, I wrote this book using the mini-habit of writing 333 words each day. On some days, I wrote more, lots more. But once I made my mini-habit, I never missed a day without writing at least 333 words. Soon enough, it became second nature and the project was complete far sooner than I ever could have imagined.

"What you do every day matters far more than what you do every now and again."

— Author Gretchen Rubin

GETTING YOUR HAND STAMPED

BEFORE WE LEAVE THIS LENGTHY chapter, I want you to meet someone. Let's take that raft out to Tom Sawyer Island so I can introduce you to Tom Sawyer himself. Okay, there never was a *real* Tom Sawyer; he only exists in the immortal tales of Mark Twain. Instead, meet Tom Nabble, the cast member who first played Tom Sawyer as a thirteen-year-old kid in 1956. Tom's story characterizes all four of Walt's success secrets: Curiosity, Confidence, Courage, and Consistency.

Growing up in Orange County, Tom was naturally *curious* about the park being built in his backyard. Tom had a paper route and would go to the site to watch construction and then sell papers to employees at the ends of their shifts. Tom wasn't a celebrity or a member of the press, but he did manage to make it inside Disneyland on opening day, even though he didn't have a ticket. His mom and he stood outside seeking autographs from the celebrities who had come, and Danny Thomas happily handed over his tickets to Tom when he and his wife decided to leave early.

As a result of Tom's *confident* sales skills, the company responsible for selling newspapers inside Disneyland hired Tom to be one of its newsboys. When Tom heard that Tom Sawyer Island was scheduled to open in 1956, in time for Disneyland's first full summer, he coveted the job of playing Tom Sawyer and *courageously* went looking for the man who could make that happen, Walt Disney. Tom described what then happened:

> I found Walt and told him I looked just like Tom Sawyer and he should hire me to be Tom Sawyer on the island. He didn't hire me on the spot like I had hoped. But the key thing is he didn't say "no." So that left the door open. He said that he'd think about it. Anytime I could find Walt in the park, I would ask him if he were still thinking about it. He finally said, "You know, I could put a mannequin...or was it a dummy? I could put a mannequin, I think it was, that wouldn't be leaving every five minutes for a hot dog and a Coke.

It took months of *constant* pestering, but one day, while playing pinball in the Disneyland arcade, Tom was called over to the Rivers of America for a meeting. "Are you still interested in working here as Tom Sawyer?" Walt asked. "You bet," was Tom's *confident* response.

Over the next five years, Tom worked on the island, playing out his dream as Tom Sawyer. He was the "Happiest Kid on Earth" until he turned eighteen and was forced to move over to operations. After all, "in Disneyland, Tom Sawyer has to stay a kid forever." Nonetheless, he managed to parlay his initial curiosity, confidence, courage, and consistency into a five-decade career with Disney, finally retiring in 2003 as the last working cast member from 1955.

Oh, by the way...when Walt Disney first hired Tom to play the part of Tom Sawyer, there was only one stipulation. Concerned about his long-term success, Walt insisted that Tom keep up his schooling.

The minimum requirement was, of course, a “C” average.

LEARNING YOUR LESSONS

"Why worry? If you've done the very best you can, worry won't make it any better."

BLACK SUNDAY

BIRTHDAYS ARE SUPPOSED TO BE special. This is as true for places as it is for people, at least for a place as special as Disneyland. Like our own years, some birthdays at Disneyland are bigger than others. At a minimum, cast members will gather around the flagpole in Town Square on Main Street, USA around 2:30 p.m. each July 17th. An audio recording of Walt's opening day dedication speech, etched in stone on the dedication plaque that sits at the base of the flagpole, is played throughout the park. In addition, Mickey and Minnie Mouse, along with a cast of other Disney characters, sing "Happy Birthday."

It is ironic that we commemorate July 17 with such fanfare and fondness. First, Disneyland's true opening day was July 18, 1955. This was the day Walt's dream officially opened to the general public, the big audience for whom the park was built. July 17 was simply a "press premiere" and required a special ticket only available to the media and celebrities.

Secondly, July 17, 1955 was anything *but* the great, grand opening that Walt had hoped for. The day went so badly that he went on to refer to it as "Black Sunday." What went wrong?

The easier question might be to ask, "What went right?" Not much.

History tells us that the first guest to enter Disneyland on Monday, July 18, 1955 at 10 a.m. was Dave MacPherson. I'm not sure who first walked in on July 17, but it might well have been the proverbial Mr. Murphy of Murphy's Law.

Whatever could go wrong, did go wrong.

First, we need to remember that the entire park was constructed in exactly one calendar year. Nothing like Disneyland existed anywhere else in the world. Nonetheless, in a mere twelve months, contractors were tasked with creating castles, pirate ships, riverboats, and jungle cruises out of the sleepy orange groves in what was then the middle of nowhere Southern California. It seemed an impossible task. And when the curtain opened on the grand stage of Disneyland, it initially revealed that the impossible was just that—impossible.

In front of 90 million viewers, then the largest live broadcast in television history, Walt Disney and his hosts, radio and television personality Art Linkletter, movie star Ronald Reagan (not yet President), and movie and TV star Bob Cummings led America through its first Disneyland tour. On TV, Walt's Magic Kingdom came across as a dream come true. Behind the scenes, however, it looked far more like the tale of a tragic kingdom. The litany of troubles is long, including:

Overcrowding: Six thousand special, timed tickets were issued to the invited media and celebrities. These were easily counterfeited, however, and the crowd soared to an estimated 33,000. Making matters worse, no one ensured that guests adhered to their scheduled times either for entry or exit. The park was woefully understaffed and understocked, quickly running out of food and drink.

Plumbers' Strike: Due to an Orange County plumbers' strike that was only settled a few days before opening, not enough laborers were available to finish all of the park's plumbing needs. Walt had to make a choice: toilets or drinking fountains? He opted for toilets with the rationalization that "You can drink Coke and Pepsi but they can't pee in the street."

Weather: July 17 was an exceptionally hot day, even for mid-summer in Southern California. Temperatures soared above 100 degrees, with official ceremonies scheduled to get underway in the heat of the afternoon. The weather only exacerbated the shortage of drinks at the concession areas and the lack of drinking fountains throughout the park.

Incomplete Construction: Walt once promised that, "Disneyland will never be finished." This was exceptionally true on opening day. It was evident even on Main Street where construction crews had raced to pour asphalt that very morning; thus, it did not have time to dry fully. Women, wearing the standard high heels of the 1950s, found their shoes sticking in the soft goo. Some of them purchased moccasins—the only adult-size shoes for sale in the park—as replacements.

Safety: So many guests tried to board the *Mark Twain* Riverboat at the same time that it began listing to one side. Water from the Rivers of America drew even with the boat, risking a near *Titanic*-sized disaster. A gas leak developed in Fantasyland, forcing it and the adjacent Tomorrowland and Frontierland, to close for a period of time.

Reviews the following day were anything but kind. Newspapers readily reported that Walt's dream was more nightmare than reality. In his autobiography, Disney employee Marty Sklar recalls some of the newspaper headlines and review criticisms that Walt woke up to the following morning:

> "Walt's Dream is a nightmare—a fiasco the like of which I cannot recall in thirty years of show life."
>
> "Crowds gripe over long waiting lines everywhere— Disneyland, Orange County's new $17 million playground, was a land of gripes and complaints again today, as a huge, milling throng of 48,000 [sic] people had the place bulging at the seams."

> "The opening was a confused mess. The first headache was the bumper-to-bumper traffic for seven miles before reaching the park, dubbed 'the worst traffic mess we've ever seen' by police."
>
> "Many citizens of Anaheim are beginning to regard the opening of Disneyland with dismay and 'mixed emotions'—the kind the man had when he pushed his mother-in-law over the cliff in his new Cadillac."

In fact, the press was so bad that Walt immediately went to work to set things right and ensured that each reporter received a special invitation to return to the park and have another opportunity to experience Disneyland the way he originally envisioned and intended.

Walt had done his best, but this time, that hadn't been good enough. Rather than let it defeat him, Walt never forgot this lesson. From that day forward, the company began the practice of "soft openings." A soft opening allows new shows, attractions, or even entire parks to become operational slowly and in front of a small and select audience. This practice gives the opportunity to work out any potential kinks, bugs, etc., and perfect the experience before exposing it to the general public. This plan hasn't guaranteed that the Disneyland staff never makes a mistake, but it has certainly minimized the chances of ever having another "Black Sunday."

"it's a small world"

PART OF THE CHALLENGE WITH Disneyland's opening day wasn't just the constraint of time but also the constraint of money. The original four-million-dollar estimate quickly mushroomed into seventeen million dollars, and that was without finishing everything Walt desired for Disneyland at its opening. Walt had hoped to secure financing through corporate sponsors, but not many were willing to risk the venture. Nothing like Disneyland yet existed anywhere else in the world, so most bankers had a strong aversion to that kind of risk. Those who did sign up, like the leased stores on Main Street, did so with only a five-year commitment. When asked, the store owners would honestly say that they believed the park, and their investment, would be gone in less than one year.

Fast-forward nine years. In 1964, New York, home to many of the banks and corporations that initially didn't believe in Disneyland, was hosting the World's Fair. This time around, its planners came to Walt, asking for his help and wisdom in building attractions that would lure visitors and make them look good. According to Van Arsdale France, in *Window on Main Street*:

> The New York World's Fair of 1964 was in trouble. The Fair committee needed a master showman to bring life and excitement to a project which seemed a bit dull. The promoters turned to Walt Disney, and he drove a hard bargain. He agreed to design four attractions, provided that he could bring them to Disneyland after the Fair closed.

Never one to gloat, Walt jumped at the chance to help the World's Fair. According to Bob Thomas in *Walt Disney: An American Original*, Walt said, "We've proved we can do it with Disneyland.... This is a great opportunity for us to grow. We can use their financing to develop a lot of technology that will help us in the future. And we'll be getting new attractions for Disneyland, too."

Using the infusion of newfound money, the Imagineers got busy. The result was an investment in theme park technology that propelled the park into its next decade and beyond. Below is a brief description of each of Walt's World's Fair Attractions, a brief description of its show, how it was incorporated into Disneyland, and the number of guests who viewed it in New York:

Ford Motors & The Magic Skyway (15 million guests): Visitors were transported through history via Ford vehicles. The technology from this attraction morphed into multiple attractions at Disneyland, including the Primeval World (Disneyland Railroad between Tomorrowland and Main Street Stations) and Tomorrowland's Peoplemover.

General Electric & Progressland (16 million guests): A unique, circular theatre that constantly revolved, allowing 250 guests to enter and exit simultaneously while other patrons enjoyed the ongoing show. Using four acts, Progressland told the story of progress through a century of electricity. The show would move to Disneyland's new Tomorrowland in 1967 and then on to Walt Disney World in 1975 where it remains today. Hourly capacity is 3,600 guests.

State of Illinois & Great Moments with Mr. Lincoln (attendance unknown): Taking the technology from the recently opened Enchanted Tiki Room, Imagineers developed the first full-sized audio-animatronic figure in the form of America's sixteenth President, and Walt's boyhood hero, Abraham Lincoln. Eventually, the technology from this attraction would grow into a full-sized Hall of Presidents in Walt Disney World's Liberty Square in 1971.

Pepsi-Cola & "it's a small world" (10.3 million guests): Nine months before the Fair's opening, Pepsi asked Walt for help in developing an attraction that would pay tribute to the children of the world and support the United Nations International Children's Emergency Fund (UNICEF). "it's a small world" made famous the Sherman Brothers' song that now holds the world's record as the most frequently played in music history. Today, every Disney park has a version of "it's a small world", but the original from the New York World's Fair came home to Disneyland in 1966. The technology for Walt's "little boat ride" was replicated in the last attraction that he personally worked on, Pirates of the Caribbean, an attraction originally imagined as a wax museum walkthrough.

Beyond the attractions themselves, the 1964 World's Fair inspired many of Walt's ideas for what would become his Experimental Prototype Community of Tomorrow or EPCOT. During their run at the fair over the course of two six-month intervals, the above attractions hosted millions of guests, and all four were highly ranked, proving that the East Coast also had a voracious appetite for Disney-style theme park entertainment, making possible the official announcement of Walt's "Florida Project" in 1965.

LIFE'S NOT FAIR

WE WOULD ALL DO WELL to learn our lessons from each and every experience, be they positive or negative. Too often, we believe that the only good in life comes from what goes according to plan and meets our expectations. In truth, we learn far more from our failures than we do our successes.

To learn Black Sunday's lessons, we would be wise to ask, "What changed?" What did Walt do to turn things around in such short order that, as cited by Bob Thomas in *Walt Disney: An American Original,* "within seven weeks, a million visitors had come to Disneyland. Predictions of attendance had been exceeded by 50 percent, and customers were spending 30 percent more money than had been expected"?

In his best-selling book, *The Success Principles,* Jack Canfield starts by challenging his readers upfront, in Chapter One, to take 100 percent responsibility for their lives. "If you want to be successful, you have to take 100% responsibility for everything that you experience in your life. This includes the level of your achievements, the results you produce, the quality of your relationships, the state of your health and physical fitness, your income, your debts, your feelings—everything!" Canfield then readily admits, "This is not easy."

It is easy to blame the prevailing culture of entitlement, a culture that runs counter to the realities of 100 percent responsibility, for why success is so difficult and taking responsibility is so evasive. In truth, more is at play here than mindless millennials looking for escape and excuses. Our tendency toward blame rather than responsibility is at the core of what it means to be human. We are simply wired this way. But if you are going to learn your lessons and take your life to a higher level, you must avoid the temptation of natural tendencies.

Whenever you are enjoying a success or fighting through a failure, regardless of outcome, you will need to account for what researchers call attribution theory. According to Shane Snow in *Smartcuts: How Hackers, Innovators, and Icons Accelerate Success,* attribution theory identifies the natural tendency of people to explain both success and failure "by attributing them to factors that will allow them to feel as good as possible about themselves." When you experience a success, it is because of something you inherently did: You worked hard. You possessed the right talent. Your special skill set made the difference.

Failure, however, is a different story. At least that's the story we tell ourselves, and hey, it's our lie, so we can tell it any way we want! Human nature demands that we attribute our failures not to ourselves (remember, the goal here is to feel okay with ourselves at the end of the day) but to external factors we readily recognize as being *beyond* our control. For example:

1. "The referee made a bad call."
2. "My boss is an idiot."
3. "My spouse doesn't support me."
4. "No one ever really believed in me."

The primary problem with attribution isn't that it's not normal or natural. It is. The challenge is that it blinds us from taking our first critical step toward success…taking 100 percent responsibility.

You can't learn your lessons with an attitude of attribution. Let's go back to Walt Disney, Disneyland, and Black Sunday. Hindsight being 20/20, we now know that external factors played a huge role in the disaster that was Disneyland's first day. Note, however, that we never, not once, hear Walt blaming God for the weather (100-plus degree heat), plumbers for going on strike (no drinking fountains), the crowds for crashing the gates with counterfeit tickets, construction crews for rides breaking down, or the potential catastrophe that was the gas leak in Fantasyland. Each of these episodes represents a legitimate, external excuse for why Black Sunday became Black Sunday.

Instead, Walt did what you need to do. He *took responsibility*. Instead of looking for blame, he set out seeking solutions. Whatever he could fix, he did. And whatever was out of the realm of his control (the heat wave lasted an interminable two weeks), he simply let go and moved on with his dream.

In *Window on Main Street*, Van Arsdale France, a recipient of one of the hallowed "Windows on Main Street" and a member of Club 55, a club named for the year the park opened that honors cast members who worked Black Sunday, shares his observations regarding Walt and the work he did to find solutions: "If it hadn't been for Walt, the odds are that the doomsayers who predicted spectacular failure would have been right. But, he seemed to thrive on the challenges. He said, 'I function better when things are going badly than when they're as smooth as whipped cream.' If he had designed the challenges, they couldn't have been much tougher."

"It is good to have a failure while you're young because it teaches you so much. For one thing it makes you aware that such a thing can happen to anybody, and once you've lived through the worst, you're never quite as vulnerable afterward."

— Walt Disney

SOUVENIR STOP

OKAY. YOU'VE MADE A MISTAKE, maybe two. Congratulations! You have officially joined the human race and demonstrated that you are at least trying. Where do we go from here?

Take Responsibility—Take a moment and list either your biggest or most recent mistake. Write down below what you, and you alone, are responsible for in what went wrong. Don't attribute any of the errors to other people or external factors. Focus on taking responsibility for your action or inaction and your choices and decisions that brought you your end result.

____

____

____

____

____

____

____

____

____

Learn Your Lesson—Again, we learn more from our mistakes than we do from our successes. Write down three lessons you can learn from the above mistake. How can you take this lesson to heart and apply it in all future endeavors?

1. ____

____

2. ____

____

3. ____

____

Give Yourself a Break—Now that you have taken 100 percent responsibility and learned your lesson, your last step is simply to let it go and walk away. If necessary, write a quick note of forgiveness to yourself. Worrying about it and beating yourself up over it isn't going to change the past or propel you into a better or brighter future. Give yourself credit for trying, and know that you can, and will, do better next time.

GETTING YOUR HAND STAMPED

AT THE BEGINNING OF THIS chapter, I noted that we don't celebrate birthdays equally. Some are bigger than others. Disneyland's first big birthday bash came on its "Tencennial," July 17, 1965. As part of the grand celebration, Great Moments with Mr. Lincoln moved into the Main Street Opera House. The World's Fair was still running in New York, however, so this audio-animatronic figure was actually the second Mr. Lincoln.

Wait, number two? Why did Walt decide to build two Mr. Lincolns?

According to Bob Thomas in *Walt Disney: An American Original*, the first audio-animatronic Lincoln was created at the Disney studio in Burbank. Upon completion "the winkin' blinkin' Lincoln" worked flawlessly and was only then flown three thousand miles east for his New York engagement. When he arrived, however, he hardly worked at all. Some of the Imagineers feared that Abe was suffering from jetlag, but most suspected errant electricity currents, especially with Shea Stadium opening nearby and the Mets playing night games. Remembering the disaster of Black Sunday, Walt refused to open the show, but he still found himself, once again, apologizing to the press, "There isn't going to be any show.... We've worked like beavers to get it ready, but it's not ready, and I won't show it to you until it is."

Walt had learned his lesson. So much so that he eventually had a second Lincoln built and stationed below the stage of the original as a stand-in "just in case." Fortunately, he was never needed and thus available to Disneyland in 1965 during the World Fair's second season.

"Experience is the name everyone gives to their mistakes."

— Oscar Wilde

BUILDING A BERM

"I don't want the public to see the world they live in while they're in the park (Disneyland). I want them to feel they're in another world."

WHAT IS A BERM?

DISNEYLAND HAS DEVELOPED A WORLDWIDE fanatical following. This result is amazing, especially in light of the original Disneyland doomsayers who predicted the park to be "Walt's Folly." Of course, many said the same regarding *Snow White and the Seven Dwarfs,* so technically Disneyland would have been "Walt's Folly 2." I love *Snow White,* but I would argue this story is one of those rare instances when the sequel is actually better than the original.

Despite the fears and cries of folly, Walt was right. Of course, Walt was right. Walt was right because he didn't build "just" an amusement park. Walt was right because he was exploring a new medium of entertainment that he knew his audience would be more than eager to experience.

Walt never allowed the disdain of his critics to distract him from his dreams, "We are not trying to entertain the critics. I'll take my chances with the public." Long before the critics climbed onboard and the media made sense of it all, Disneyland made a magical, emotional connection with the masses. By September 1955, a million guests had already visited. Today, as Disneyland prepares for its 60th birthday, it is proud to proclaim that it has played host to well over 650 million guests over these past six decades. At first, the financiers couldn't figure it out. Bankers didn't get it. So-called "experts" were convinced the public would be equally puzzled. Walt once said, "I could never convince the financiers that Disneyland was feasible because dreams offer too little collateral."

The financiers were wrong.

The so-called experts were wrong. Walt was right.

If you are curious enough, curious in the way Walt and the park encourage you to be, then at some point, you will want to extend your enjoyment into explanation. You will start asking questions. You will want to know more. Your desire to make the intangibles tangible will create an insatiable inquiry for how the park works. What is it *exactly* that makes Disneyland so special? How exactly do the Imagineers make all this magic? Like any good magician, the Magic Kingdom doesn't readily share its secrets. And why should it? In many ways, those secrets are for our own protection. Disneyland is like a baby's rattle. If you bust the rattle open to try to learn how it works, you end up breaking the rattle, thus muting the magic. Oops! There is one obvious Disneyland secret that I feel safe in sharing. It is okay to let you in on this because if you have ever been to Disneyland, then you have already seen it. If you've never been, then let me encourage you to pull up an image of Disneyland on Google Earth and play along.

Disneyland works because Walt had the wisdom to build a berm. I know what you are thinking. "A berm? I don't even know what a berm is, but somehow you are telling me that I've already seen one?" Yes. Yes, I am.

Blogger Randy Crane, at www.leavingconformitycoaching. com, sees the berm, an artificial hill that encircles Disneyland, as Walt's masterful idea to control the view for Disneyland's guests. To really be "in" Disneyland means to be inside the confines of the berm. If you're not looking for it, you'll probably never notice it, but it's there, serving that very important purpose. In describing the berm in *The Vatican to Vegas,* Norman Klein says, "Technically a berm was a shoulder of earth that obscured Anaheim from visitors."

Remember how Walt wanted a flat canvas, a piece of land where he could forge his own rivers, make his own mountains, and create his own castle? Be careful what you wish for. Once cleared, Walt realized his canvas, i.e., his 160 Anaheim acres, was *too* flat. As a moviemaker, he was accustomed to having complete control of his set or soundstage. The dynamics of the real world aren't nearly as pliable. The solution came by building a berm—a method of screening the park and the public from the real world—by surrounding the perimeter with twenty feet of raised earth. The 350 tons of dirt necessary for building the berm came from dredging the Rivers of America, Frontierland's centerpiece waterway. Sam Gennawey writes in *The Disneyland Story,* "If Walt wanted to take his guests to the American Wilderness or the African jungle, he needed to make sure people were not seeing a freeway exchange, highrise buildings, or transmission lines from inside the park."

BEYOND THE BERM

LIKE THE BELT ON A middle-aged man, over time, the berm has expanded along with the park. This expansion has allowed for the accommodation of additional attractions and even an entirely new area, Mickey's Toontown, just beyond the original park perimeter in Fantasyland. Nonetheless, Disneyland remains land-locked, thus requiring even more magic to accommodate new ideas and additional advancement.

Today, part of the berm's magic is how it plays tricks on your person. You can start an attraction clearly within the park's confines and perimeter, pass under the berm and into a "show building" for the actual ride, and then back under the berm for your ride exit and re-entry into Disneyland. Yes, there are times when you physically depart Disneyland, but the magic masks you from knowing it.

Examples include the Indiana Jones Adventure in Adventureland. Aside from the popularity of this attraction, part of the reason for the one-eighth-mile length queue is to get guests beyond the berm and into the enormous show building that sits on the other side. You may not realize it, but you are actually closer to the Indiana Jones attraction when you are on the eastern end of the Downtown Disney shopping district than when you are actually in Adventureland.

My favorite beyond-the-perimeter excursion is the trip you take on Pirates of the Caribbean in New Orleans Square. Initially, I believed you spent your fifteen minutes sailing beneath the Square's streets. Not true. The waterfalls at the beginning of your journey serve to plummet you below and beyond the berm. You then sail into another show building where your plundering, pirate adventure begins in earnest.

Yo ho, yo ho, beyond the berm for me!

For many guests, the stretching room in the Haunted Mansion, also in New Orleans Square, is a favorite scene. Know, however, that the stretching room isn't just for show. It also serves a much more practical purpose. As you stand in the "dead center of the room," watching the portraits betray their patrons, the elevator is taking you several feet below ground (*six feet under*, perhaps?). Once the room opens back up, you walk to your "doom buggy." Unbeknownst to many, the walk from the elevator to the loading zone is a walk underneath the Disneyland Railroad train tracks, beyond the berm, and out into another show building that sits outside the park's perimeter. You never actually ride inside the "mansion." The antebellum style house was built as a façade in 1963, but construction on the attraction part, the show building beyond the berm, didn't begin until 1967.

Lastly, there is Splash Mountain in Critter Country. For years, I tried to determine whether you ride through the mountain itself, or whether it, too, contains a show building. I would peek around the park's perimeter or stare at images on Google Earth, trying to figure it all out. I finally unmasked the magic last March.

While riding Splash Mountain with my sister, we suddenly came to a stop early on in the show, long before the famed fifty-two-foot plunge that awaits you at the end. This had *never* happened to me before. Suspiciously, this was also the first time I was riding Splash Mountain with my sister. The *same* sister who exactly forty years earlier had peed in the Tiki Room.

Hmm....

We sat languishing in our logs for several minutes, and eventually, cast members came and carefully evacuated us. When we exited out of the "mountain," it was obvious that we were actually leaving a building. Once outside, we traversed down stairs and into a backstage area that clearly sits beyond the berm. Now that I have experienced it, I can see it all clearly. Some might call it an epiphany, but I like to refer to it as my personal form of "Zip-A-Dee-Doo-DUH!"

THE POWER OF FOCUS

BUILDING THE BERM IS WHAT helped Disneyland be so successful. It is rarely noticed or appreciated by guests, but it is essential to the overall experience. The berm envelops the park and insulates you inside the magic. Building a berm can assist you in your success, too.

Focus is *power*.

Just as Walt did not want outside distractions diverting his guests' attention, you don't want distractions diverting you away from your dreams, goals, and visions. And boy, are we distracted.

Digital devices fill our days and nights. We are rarely, if ever, unplugged. Walt built his berm years before cellphones, the Internet, Facebook, or Twitter. Nonetheless, perhaps Walt was wise to the words of the poet T.S. Eliot, "We are distracted from distractions by distractions."

Remember our opening story? The one where Walt is sitting alone on a park bench with only peanuts to keep him company? Imagine for a moment what that scene might look like today. Can you picture yourself sitting on that same bench with your mind engaged, and *only* engaged, with your ideas and your imagination? Probably not.

When I see myself sitting there, I see myself plugged into my cellphone. We live in a world where we can't just "be." Instead, we are constantly seeking outside validation via our Facebook posts, Twitter accounts, and email messages. "Walt unplugged" is the Walt that came up with the idea for Disneyland. We need to start building berms, especially between our technology and ourselves. Otherwise, we will always be plugged in. Always be distracted. Technology will drown out our innermost thoughts and ideas, crush our creativity, and doom us to a life and world of status quo.

A DAY THAT WILL LIVE IN INFAMY

One December night at dinner, while my daughter Bethany was still in middle school, I did what most parents do around the dinner table—I asked about her day at school. She shared that they played volleyball in P.E., worked on problems in pre-algebra, and wrote an essay in history. Hearing the word "history" piqued my interest, so I immediately inquired further. "What did you write your essay on in history?" I asked.

"Oh, the importance and significance of December 7," she replied. "Wow, you got to write an essay on the bombing of Pearl Harbor and America's entry into World War II," her U.S. history teacher dad responded. "That's great!"

After several seconds of silence, I looked up and realized Bethany was whiter than the paint on Space Mountain. "What's wrong?" I asked.

Pushing back tears, she responded, "I didn't write my essay on the bombing of Pearl Harbor."

"Okay," I replied. "Well, for the love of God and all things holy, if you didn't write your history essay on the importance of December 7 as the date of the bombing of Pearl Harbor, then what *did* you write about?"

She responded with words that only a seventh grade girl can understand. "I wrote my essay on the upcoming middle school dance. It's this Friday, December 7th, and they've been announcing it all week."

Mortified, she immediately went to work writing a new essay and turned it into her teacher first thing the following morning. I, of course, have had fun with it ever since. As a history teacher, I still recognize December 7th as Pearl Harbor Day, but now it is also "Middle School Dance Day" for our family. Each year, I give Bethany a "Middle School Dance Day" card (not easy to find) and even have my college-level U.S. History students sign it for her.

If we allow it, the dance of life can quickly distract us from what's really important, just as a middle school dance distracted my daughter from realizing the significance of World War II. That said, we all have to participate in the dance of life, so in order to take your dreams seriously, you must choose focus as your dance partner. We always get more of what we focus on, so build your berm and get serious about what you allow in and what you keep out. In his book *The Success Principles,* Jack Canfield reminds us of the importance of focus, "Everything you think, say, and do needs to become intentional and aligned with your purpose, your values and your goals." Disneyland's berm serves as a similar reminder.

"The berm creates your horizon and helps you define what belongs in your experience and what doesn't."

— Randy Crane

CHOOSE YOUR FOCUS

WALT DISNEY WAS A MAN who brought immense joy to billions of people around the world, especially children. Many are surprised to learn, however, that Walt had anything but a happy childhood. He spent a lifetime living his dreams while also being chased by nightmares.

Most painful were his memories from Kansas City, Missouri, where he worked for his father, without pay, delivering newspapers for six years from the ages of nine to fifteen. Like a mailman, Walt delivered in all kinds of weather, including soaking rainstorms and arctic-like blizzards. In order to meet the newspaper delivery truck by 4:30 a.m., Walt was up at 3:30 a.m., every morning. According to Jim Korkis in *The Revised Vault of Walt*, "Walt had recurrent nightmares throughout his life, and one of them was that he had missed customers on his section of the paper route. He'd wake up in a kind of a cold sweat and think, 'Gosh, I've got to hurry and get back. My dad will be waiting up at that corner.'"

Aside from the Midwestern elements, Walt Disney also had to deal with the obvious economic disparity between his cashstrapped family and the customers on his route who were far better off financially. Korkis writes about Walt and his paper route:

> The kids would leave their toys out on the porch after playing with them the previous evening. Walt didn't have any toys.... Everything his parents gave him was practical, like underwear or a winter jacket.... At 5:00 a.m., in the dark, Walt would put his sack of papers down and play with his wind-up trains and other toys. He'd sit there and play all alone with them. Once, he came to a porch where he found toys and a box of half-eaten candy. So he sat there and ate some of the half-eaten candy and played with the toys.

Having a difficult upbringing does not make Walt special or unique. On some level, we all have our own special form of childhood trauma.

The difference is *focus*.

Over the years, Walt managed to build a berm around his childhood. He chose the items that were useful and used them as focal points for moving forward. At the same time, he successfully shielded himself from the memories that would only serve to distract and detract him from his goals and ambitions, as Williams and Denney explain in *How to Be Like Walt*:

> Walt's boyhood years are instructive because of the way he chose to deal with his childhood memories. He spoke with heartbreaking candor about having nightmares throughout his life, yet he never let childhood pain darken his optimism. Walt chose to focus on the good in life while letting go of the bad. He shaped his life around warm, nostalgic memories of Marceline, the romance of the railroad, the thrill of his first circus parade, the joy of seeing *Snow White* on the silver screen. He chose to emulate his father's positive traits while disregarding the negative traits.

Focus is a powerful force. When we focus, we are saying "Yes" to what we think is important and "No" to what we choose to make irrelevant. Building a berm around who we are and where we are going will enable us to bring the focus necessary for achieving any goal or realizing any dream.

"Focus is about saying no."

— Steve Jobs

SOUVENIR STOP

Successful people know how to make choices. Recognize that when you say "Yes" to one thing, and focus accordingly, you are simultaneously saying "No" to all of the other options. Let's ask ourselves some questions:

1. **Picture your life as the empty canvas Walt started with in Anaheim**. What, exactly, do you wish to fill your world with? What do you want more of that would help your days feel special,

magical, and more memorable? Remember, you always get more of whatever it is you *choose* to focus on. List these now.

____

____

____

____

2. **Saying "Yes" to what you want requires you to say "No" to anything that distracts you from what you truly want.** What do you want less of? These items go outside of your berm. List them below.

____

____

____

____

3. **Build your berm by training your brain to focus.** How many focused minutes per day can you give to your dreams? Even if you can only start with five minutes, know that your berm, like Disneyland's, can build over time. Your brain is like any other muscle, so start training it by finding a quiet, distraction-free place where you only work on something you want more of and you exclude all distractions and everything you say you want less of. Again, start with five minutes each day and build from there. Commit to a time and place by writing them below:

Place: ______________________ Time: ____________

GETTING YOUR HAND STAMPED

NUMEROUS SOURCES TESTIFY THAT WALT Disney was so focused on the guest experience at Disneyland that he would often stand at the park's exit and ask people about their day. As he was walking in one afternoon, hours before the park's closing, he came across a family who was already heading out. Leaving Disneyland early was a rarity back in those days so Walt stopped them and inquired about their early exit. "We could see the interstate from the Skyway and want to get out before the traffic hits," they told him.

This response became part of Walt's inspiration for Walt Disney World. Disneyland has the blessing of the berm, but Disney World has the blessing of a buffer, property equivalent in size to the island of Manhattan. In Florida, guests travel some five miles through wooded Disney property before ever reaching the parking lot of Walt Disney World's Magic Kingdom. From there, you are still two miles away from Main Street with Seven Seas Lagoon between you and your destination. The berm at Disneyland vs. the buffer at Walt Disney World is part of the reason why Imagineer Tony Baxter, in a television interview, once said, "Disneyland hugs you but Walt Disney World swallows you."

What kind of world are you trying to create? Don't let your success get swallowed up by your distractions. Embrace your dreams and know that protecting them is a necessary step for creating your magical life.

MAKING A MAIN STREET IMPRESSION

"What you need is a wienie, which says to people 'come this way.' People won't go down a long corridor unless there's something promising at the end. You have to have something that beckons them to 'walk this way.'"

MAIN STREET MEMORIES

EVER THE ENTERTAINER, WALT DISNEY understood the importance of starting a show with a strong opening. Disneyland was Walt's ultimate show and Main Street is the park's opening act. Walt knew that if he could "hook" his audience on Main Street, they would continue to explore the rest of the park and return again for multiple visits. In *The Disneyland Story,* Sam Gennawey suggests that we think of Main Street as Disneyland's "opening statement" because during its development, "every detail had been subject to Walt's scrutiny."

Main Street stands as a testament to America at the crossroads of the nineteenth and twentieth centuries, an in-between era of technologies: the gas lamp vs. the electric light, the horse and buggy vs. the streetcar. Gennawey recalls that Walt promised, "For those of us who remember the carefree times it re-creates, Main Street will bring back happy memories. For younger visitors, it is an adventure in turning back the calendar to the days of grandfather's youth."

Main Street may not provide us with the E-ticket, thrill ride memories so many of us crave in our twenty-first century world. Nonetheless, Main Street still leaves a lasting impression. Guests rarely remember walking into Adventureland, Frontierland, Fantasyland, or Tomorrowland for the first time. You almost always, however, remember your first time on Main Street.

When a colleague of mine heard about my History of Disneyland class and this book project, she was excited to share with me a story from her very first trip to Disneyland. It was the mid-1960s, and my friend, Gail, was still a young child. Her father was a marine serving in the Vietnam War and the family was living at Camp Pendleton, south of Anaheim. One afternoon, a bus came to the base and picked up all of the families who had loved ones serving overseas. The bus' destination was kept a surprise. Gail's heart leapt when she saw the snowcapped Matterhorn Mountain from the Santa Ana Freeway. She was finally going to Disneyland!

Nearly fifty years later, Gail's memories don't include any rides, shows, or attractions. All she talks about is how beautiful and magical Main Street was. "I had pictured it in my dreams, but nothing in my imagination could compare to the real thing." That night, Disneyland treated everyone on her bus to a free serving of ice cream at the Gibson Girl Ice Cream Parlor. "It was, and is, the best ice cream I have ever tasted. Sitting there that night, even with my father in harm's way half-way across the world, everything was okay...as long as we stayed there, on Main Street."

WHAT IS A "WIENIE"?

WHO WOULDN'T WANT TO STAY there—on Main Street? Actually, staying on Main Street is the last thing Walt wanted when he built his single-street entrance into Disneyland. He wanted Main Street to give guests their first impression, but certainly not their last. Main Street serves as the opening scene to a much bigger story. Sleeping

Beauty Castle stands at the end of Main Street as not just the gateway into Fantasyland but as Main Street's "wienie." What in the world is a "wienie"?

In *The Revised Vault of Walt,* Disney historian Jim Korkis writes that Walt "was an amazingly complex and an amazingly simple man." His simplicity is best seen through his taste buds. Walt was a simple eater. His favorite food was chili. When he ate alone at his studio in Burbank, "he would combine a can of Gebhardt's (which had much meat and few beans) with a can of Dennison's (which had less meat but more beans)." Furthermore, Walt found hot dogs irresistible. Except that he didn't call them hot dogs. Instead, he referred to them as "wienies," a word he learned in his childhood. At the end of the day, he would enter his home through the kitchen so he could sneak two cold, raw hot dogs from the refrigerator, one for him and one for his small white poodle. Sam Gennawey, in *The Disneyland Story,* states, "By wiggling the treat, Walt could get his dog to go from side to side, around in a circle, jump up and more. Wherever he moved the wienie, his dog would eagerly follow. Both Walt and the dog loved the game and she was finally rewarded with the tasty and satisfying treat."

Walt took the simple hot dog and turned it into something more architecturally complex in Disneyland. After his guests' introduction to Disneyland by way of a Main Street first impression, Walt then needed to get them to go where he wanted them to go. Ever the director, Walt devised a "wienie" in each land as a way to lure guests and get them to follow. Sleeping Beauty Castle and the view of the King Arthur Carrousel serves this purpose for Main Street and Fantasyland. Once you reached the central hub, the original TWA Moonliner was the wienie for Tomorrowland to your right and the mighty *Mark Twain* Riverboat was the wienie for Frontierland to your left. What about Adventureland? Adventureland has no wienie, only a mysterious bend that beckons you around the corner, and that is part of the adventure!

Leadership and success are wrapped in a variety of layers. One of the most crucial layers lies in your ability to influence people and inspire them to move in a certain direction. Like Main Street, you want to make a good, lasting first impression.

This is only your opening act, however.

People then need a compelling reason to remain interested and to "come this way," knowing that more excitement and adventure are sure to follow.

NOT JUST ANY STREET, U.S.A.

Walt Disney was born in Chicago, Illinois, in 1901. His father, Elias, built the home in which Walt was born as well as several others on the same block. This was a rare period of success for Elias, but he eventually grew tired of the big city. As Chicago grew, so did Elias' fears about its corrupting influence on his young children. In 1906, with money Elias had saved as a Chicago contractor, Elias and Flora purchased a forty-five-acre farm near Marceline, Missouri. According to Williams and Denney in *How to Be Like Walt*, "this move profoundly affected Walt's life. He would later recall nothing of those early Chicago years; his earliest memories were those of a Missouri farm boy."

Unable to make a living as a Midwestern, Missouri farmer, Elias, now in failing health, decided to move the family, again, in 1910. Although he only lived there less than five years, Walt always considered himself a Marceline boy. So much so that when it came time for him to build Disneyland, it was his memories of Marceline that inspired the design of Main Street, U.S.A. In *The Vault of Walt: Volume 2*, Jim Korkis states, "It was in Marceline that Walt experienced his first film, his first theatrical stage production, his first circus, and his first interaction with live farm animals. Walt attempted his first drawings in Marceline. All of these things—and more—made a lasting impression on him."

While Main Street, U.S.A. harkens back to Walt Disney's childhood in Marceline, others see Fort Collins, Colorado, as the archetype for Disneyland's Main Street. Harper Goff was the lead Imagineer who designed Main Street, and he had spent his youth in Fort Collins.

A lot of mystique surrounds Main Street, U.S.A. Arguing the point, Marceline versus Fort Collins, misses this mystique. Main Street, U.S.A. is an exact replication of neither. Instead, the imagery of Main Street is intended to tap into the idea of a "shared American experience." It is not the single memory of a single town but rather a collection of memories and symbols. In *Walt Disney's America,* Christopher Finch remarks:

> [Disney] thought in archetypes and so he conceived an idealized version of the past in which everything is as it should have been. He understood very well that nostalgia tends to blur images. What he did was to take those misty images and give them a renewed sharpness of detail that was well researched and faithful to its sources, but which eliminated imperfections and evidence of decay.

In other words, Main Street is not about a place but rather an *idea.* Main Street, U.S.A. symbolizes emotional truth far more than it represents actual reality. Thus, it wasn't the amount of time that Walt spent in Marceline that mattered. Again, he was only there for less than five years. Rather, it was the quality of the time and his experience there that left such a deep and long-lasting impression. According to Williams and Denney in *How to Be Like Walt,* Walt would one day say about Marceline: "To tell the truth, more things of importance happened to me in Marceline than have happened since—or are likely to in the future...I'm glad I'm a small-town boy and I'm glad Marceline was my town."

Just as Marceline left an impression on Walt, and Main Street, U.S.A. leaves an impression on us, we should each aspire to leave lasting impressions wherever we go. Marceline obviously influenced Walt, and we can see this influence in his life and in his park. Leadership is about influence, so we always need to consider the lasting impression we are leaving with people.

OUR OPENING ACT

WHEN NIKI AND I MARRIED, we went to Disneyland for our honeymoon. I was excited that we would be there for a full five days. Thinking back to her days working at Kings Dominion in Virginia, Niki was a bit bewildered at what we could possibly do at an amusement park for five whole days. I asked her to trust me (if she could trust me enough to marry me, I figured she could at least trust me with five days at Disneyland for a honeymoon).

Fortunately, she was enthralled the second we stepped into the park on a late August afternoon and walked onto Main Street. We started by riding the railroad around the Magic Kingdom, employing it as the preview reel that Walt originally intended. From that perspective, Niki was able to see what the next five days held for her, and she quickly realized that Disneyland wasn't really like Kings Dominion at all. We wrapped up that first night by sitting on the shore of the Rivers of America and taking in the spectacular, outdoor pyrotechnic show, Fantasmic, via premiere seating and the outstanding dessert buffet. We also rode what I believe is Disneyland's most impressive attraction, at least for a newcomer, The Indiana Jones Adventure. Niki walked out of the park that night wondering why we were *only* spending five days at Disneyland.

The most memorable moment of that magical week came the following evening. We enjoyed lunch that day at the Blue Bayou located inside the Pirates of the Caribbean. A big lunch midday freed us up in the evening to experience the fireworks on Main Street without having to worry about dinner at any particular hour. We stood there on Main Street that night looking skyward with the fireworks exploding above us. We had both seen fireworks before, and unlike Niki, I had even seen them at Disneyland. These were different.

The fireworks were now coordinated with projections on the castle and confetti cascading down from the lampposts on Main Street. Neither one of us had ever experienced anything like it. Between the lights, the people, the paper, and the serendipity of it all, Niki and I were carried away by emotion. We were madly in love with each other. And yes, it is natural for a couple to expect fireworks on their honeymoon. But to have ours come from Disneyland, on Main Street, left us both with a memorable impression that has lasted over these many years since.

SOUVENIR STOP

MAIN STREET, U.S.A. TEACHES US the importance of introductions and creating compelling reasons for people to keep moving in our direction. How can you do this at work? How can you do this at home? What kind of Main Street Memories are you making with your spouse? Your kids? Your team? Like Walt in Marceline, it isn't about the amount of time so much as it is the quality. Let's explore the following:

REMEMBER THE REALITY OF FIRST Impressions—Like it or not, people make all sorts of judgments within seconds of meeting you. Just like the details on Main Street matter, so do your clothing, grooming, and accessories. Are you confident these are communicating exactly what you want to be saying about yourself? You only have one chance, and a few seconds at that, to make a good impression. Make sure you are maximizing these opportunities each and every time.

BANK ON DEPOSITS, NOT WITHDRAWALS—FOR years, Main Street, U.S.A. housed the only bank (Bank of America) in the United States open on Sundays and holidays. Use it as your inspiration for treating every interaction with another individual as a transaction. We make deposits by being positive, easy to work with, and giving our undivided attention. We make withdrawals when we are negative, difficult, and easily distracted by other people or other things we consider obviously more important. Leave people feeling energized from having spent time with you, not exhausted.

Be Yourself—While trying to make that good, lasting impression, we would be wise to remember the words of Oscar Wilde, "Be yourself, everyone else is taken." Don't forget to be your true self at work and at home. *You* are who they hired. *You* are who they married. Make sure it is *you* who shows up every day. Be comfortable with who you really are, and know that this kind of authenticity will stand the test of time. Despite spending the majority of his life and career in Los Angeles, Walt never forgot who he really was, a Midwestern farm boy from the Main Street of Marceline, Missouri.

GETTING YOUR HAND STAMPED

One of my favorite Disneyland stories, recounted by Marty Sklar in *Dream It! Do It!*, comes from the 1960s. A Texan was standing on Main Street and surveying the Fantasy in the Sky fireworks show. Being from Texas, the man boasted that, "the show was nice, but we have 'em bigger down home." A lady standing nearby heard his boast and quietly asked, "Every night?"

The second we walk through the train station tunnels and onto Main Street, U.S.A., we feel transported to a different time and place. This is the magic that is Main Street.

We always feel special.

We feel special *every* time.

This is not a first day or first date proposition. You too can leave a Main Street Impression. *Every* day and *every* night.

USING FORCED PERSPECTIVE

"Happiness is a state of mind.
It's just according to the way you look at things."

THE ARCHITECTURE OF REASSURANCE

WHEN YOU STEP INTO DISNEYLAND, everything is not exactly as it appears. This is part of the magic. Not the magic of pixie dust or make believe—rather, the magic of architecture. Architecture originally designed by studio craftsmen who spent years honing their craft as storytellers and model makers.

Walt insisted that Disneyland be built on a scale. Part of this originated from his love for the railroad. Growing up in Marceline, Missouri, Walt had an uncle who was an engineer on the Santa Fe Railroad, Walt's first real hero. Later, Walt would go on to construct scale model trains in the backyard of his Holmby Hills home in Los Angeles. He picked up this hobby as a way to release stress from running the studio. His visit to the 1947 train expo in Chicago was a foundational experience that lay some of the "track" in Walt's mind that would one day lead to Disneyland.

Like Walt's dreams, his visions, and, ultimately, Disneyland itself, Walt's trains outgrew his backyard. The park became their new home. In essence, Disneyland is really just one giant train set. We already know that Walt was always going to build Disneyland. In addition, his Magic Kingdom was always going to have a train, a reflection of Walt's first love.

The railroad is built on a 5/8 scale. This scale provides the train, and the environment it surrounds, with a storybook essence. From there, the Imagineers designed the rest of the park using forced perspective, a piece of architectural pixie dust that tricks you into believing the buildings are larger than life. You feel taller on Main Street because the buildings, via forced perspective, appear higher than they actually are. The first floor is built to normal scale, but the second floor is built to a 3/4 scale, and the third floor at 1/2 scale. Imagineers refer to this as "the architecture of reassurance" because the perspective they create soon becomes your reality. You feel taller when standing on Main Street, U.S.A. A bit bigger. You rise up and become the hero in your own life story. You are ready to face any and every adventure that lies ahead.

What lies directly ahead is Sleeping Beauty Castle. This iconic landmark is only seventy-seven feet tall, but it appears significantly larger. How? Again, forced perspective. Like the first floors on Main Street, the bottom bricks are full scale. They shrink, however, as they climb to the castle's top. Along the way, additional design features are scaled down ending with the top spire: half the size it should be. During construction, some of Walt's staff complained that the castle was too small for the dream they were building. Walt knelt down in front of the castle and challenged his team to view it from a child's perspective.

Tucked away to the right of Sleeping Beauty Castle is another interesting piece of forced perspective, Snow White's Grotto. This is one of the more charming and quieter areas of the often otherwise busy park. The Grotto consists of ivory statues of Snow White, the Seven Dwarfs, a few woodland creatures, a bridge, and a beautiful cascading waterfall. Sometime early in the 1960s, Walt received the statue set as an anonymous gift. He loved the donation and very much wanted to incorporate it into the park. The challenge is that Snow White is carved the same size as the diminutive dwarfs. Imagineer John Hench solved this challenge by placing Snow White at the top of the waterfall and the dwarfs at ground level. This "tricks" your eyes into seeing the Snow White statue as taller than she actually is and thus sized and scaled properly in proportion to the dwarfs down below. Now you know!

Lastly, know that the buildings on Main Street, U.S.A. angle inward as you walk toward the castle. This creates the perception that the street is longer, and the castle farther away, than it actually is. You are at the beginning of your story; the day is new. The castle's distance draws you forward as you walk toward all the adventure that lies ahead. In turn, the reverse is true. As you exit the park by making your way back down Main Street, the train station now appears *closer*. You have conquered mountains and bested villains. You, the hero, are ready to head home and, thanks to the architecture of forced perspective, the Main Street Train Station, and your home beyond, appears closer than ever.

DON'T TRY THIS AT HOME

SPEAKING OF HOME, I ONCE made my own vain and veiled attempt at using the tricks of forced perspective. It ended badly for me. On my ten-year anniversary as one of the pastors at my church in Sonoma, the congregation threw me a nice, big party. I received numerous gifts and accolades, including a gift certificate for purchasing a new suit. I viewed this certificate as a commentary on my current clothing as much as a gift, but I accepted it graciously nonetheless.

The following week, I shopped for my new suit. I quickly found a salesman in Macy's and told him that I wanted a suit longer than I really am.

"Why?" he asked.

"I've heard that if you purchase a suit longer than what you really need, and you have it expertly tailored, it will make you look taller than you really are," I replied.

"Where did you hear this?" "Um, the Internet."

I have always been vertically challenged. Niki claims that, at 5' 7¾", I hail from the "Diminutive Republic." With the not-so-tacit approval of the salesman, I selected my extra long suit and headed home. While driving, I called my tailor, Tony, and shared my excitement about having a brand new suit. "Can you tailor it for me right away?" I asked. "It is a gift from my congregation, and I really want to wear it to church this Sunday."

"No problem," he replied.

I stopped at Tony the Tailor's on the way home, and he ushered me into a dressing room. Draped in my newfound finery, I walked out into the lobby looking like Tom Hanks in the last scene from the movie *Big*. The extra long suit hung on me like a curtain. Tony looked up and exclaimed, "Oh, that suit is too long! Jeff, why? Why did you buy a suit so big?"

I tried to put Tony at ease.

"Tony, don't worry about it. This is perfect! I read (on the Internet) that if you buy a suit longer than what you need, and have it tailored, which is *exactly* what you are going to do for me, Tony, then the suit will actually make you look taller."

Tony, shaking his head back and forth, responded with words I have never forgotten.

"Oh, Jeff. That suit doesn't make you look tall. That suit makes you look *stupid!*"

PERSPECTIVE IS EVERYTHING

WHILE MY ATTEMPT TO USE forced perspective to help me look taller failed, I do believe we can use the principle of forced perspective to aid us in being successful. Forced perspective isn't always about architecture. You can use forced perspective to adjust your attitude, and when it comes to life, attitude is *everything*.

Remember the story of how Walt lost Oswald, and a host of animators, early in his career? Pause for a moment and think about the implications of this story in our world today. If that happened to me, I doubt I would be looking for a new, even more successful character to replace him. Instead, I would be texting my shrink or phoning my attorney. Probably both! But Walt lived in a different world constructed with a different attitude. Not only did he come up with Mickey Mouse in the midst of his darkest moment, but he used a bit of forced perspective, aka attitude adjustment, before ever boarding the train in New York. Quoted in Timothy Susanin's *Walt Before Mickey*, the telegram Walt sent to his brother, Roy, reads like this:

> LEAVING TONIGHT STOPPING OVER KC ARRIVE HOME SUNDAY MORNING SEVEN THIRTY DON'T WORRY EVERYTHING OK WILL GIVE DETAILS WHEN ARRIVE—WALT.

Of course, we know that everything was *not* okay. In fact, quite the opposite. But Walt's attitude here reminds us of a very valuable lesson. Life is not about what happens to us. Life is always about how we respond to what happens to us. Again, think about what your reaction would be if you were standing in Walt's shoes. How would you respond after being double-crossed? Walt responded with a bit of forced perspective, and in that moment, Mickey Mouse was born:

> But was I downhearted? Not a bit! I was happy at heart. For out of the trouble and confusion stood a mocking, merry little figure. Vague and indefinite at first. But it grew and grew and grew. And finally arrived—a mouse. A rompling, rollicking little mouse.... By the time my train had reached the Middle West I had dressed my dream mouse in a pair of red velvet pants with two huge pearl buttons, had composed the first scenario and was all set.

PERSPECTIVE CAN BE PAINFUL

YOU MAY BE SURPRISED TO know that before I met my wonderful wife, Niki, I was previously married, and when that marriage came to an end, my divorce was anything but a day at Disneyland. I spent the first fourteen days of our separation in eleven different places. After an unhappy, but at least settled, marriage of twenty-three years, I now wandered from place-to-place, a nomad in the middle of the Arizona desert.

In the midst of this tumultuous time, a friend invited me to his cabin in Payson, Arizona, for a "Guy's Night." Out of options, and nearly out of cash, I readily accepted. He treated me to dinner at a local diner and then asked whether I wanted to drive out of town a few miles and go to the local casino.

I froze.

Here I was in the middle of Arizona in the middle of July—frozen. After a period of awkward silence, I blurted out, "I don't think that's a good idea."

"Why not? It will be fun! Is it a moral issue? Religion? You won't ever find anyone interested in you if you can't lighten up and have some fun!"

He wasn't going to drop it, and I had nowhere else to go, so I shared the dreaded truth.

"I have an addictive personality." "A what?" he asked.

"An addictive personality," I repeated. "What the heck does that mean?" he asked.

"In high school, I was addicted to pinball and Ms. Pac-Man. I've always avoided casinos. I know that if I ever put so much as a single nickel in a slot machine, I won't stop until I am homeless."

He looked at me and laughed. "Boy, I don't know how to tell you this. You *are* homeless!"

Ouch! Perspective can be painful!

Perspective can also bring reassurance. Reflecting back on that night, I know I learned a valuable lesson. I may have been homeless, but at least I had the shelter of friends. This lesson was worth far more than the two dollars I walked away with from the casino. Despite my "addictive personality," I've never needed to return (even with a daughter who now lives in Las Vegas). Perspective has the power of enabling us to see things any way we choose. What choice will you make?

SOUVENIR STOP

How do we build our lives so we can use the power of forced perspective to our advantage? Again, it is *not* what happens to you, but how you *respond* to what happens, that dictates your success and happiness. Your perspective plays a huge role in forming and shaping your responses. Forced perspective, the "architecture of reassurance," can be your assurance for staying on target.

Your blueprint rests in the multi-story examples we find on Main Street, U.S.A. Remember how we learned that the first floor of each building is built to full scale while the second floor is built to a 3/4 scale and the third, or top floor, is the smallest floor of all at 1/2 scale? There is a lesson here worth exploring. Using forced perspective enables us to live what I like to call "The Inverted Life." Here is how the stories in an Inverted Life stack up:

1. **First Floor (full scale)**—Gratitude, Thanksgiving, and Appreciation
2. **Second Floor (3/4 scale)**—Visions, Dreams, Goals, Successes, Aspirations, and Accomplishments
3. **Third Floor (1/2 scale)**—Problems, Challenges, Difficulties, and Obstacles

When living The Inverted Life, you recognize that gratitude goes on the ground floor. The realization of further dreams, goals, visions, and aspirations are additional stories constructed on top of your never-ending story of thankfulness and appreciation. Lastly, using forced perspective enables you to perceive the problems, challenges, difficulties, and/or obstacles you will face along the way, *and you will face them,* as significantly smaller. Suddenly, your dreams, like the castle at the end of Main Street, are now closer than they appear.

I call this The Inverted Life because most people spend their days thinking, focusing, and talking only about their problems. How much energy do you expend whining, moaning, and complaining about, well, everything? This is all waste that takes up valuable floor space. Criticism is a poor contractor for constructing an awesome life.

You always get more of whatever it is *you choose* to focus on. Instead of "tearing down," focus on "building up." Know that you are always building on top of your ground-level gratitude for what you have already received and what you have already accomplished.

Like Disneyland, Jack Canfield encourages us to have fun. In *The Success Principles,* Canfield challenges us to turn appreciation into a game: "Learn to play the Appreciation Game. Look for things to appreciate in every situation. When you actively seek the positive, you become more appreciative and optimistic, which is a requirement for creating the life of your dreams. Look for the good."

GETTING YOUR HAND STAMPED

You now know that being thankful for who you are and what you already have is foundational to building your future dreams, goals, and successes. What you may not know is the recent connection between Disneyland and the annual American Thanksgiving Holiday.

It has become customary for the President of the United States to pardon a turkey the day before Thanksgiving. Have you ever wondered what happens to the turkey after being pardoned by the President? Between 2005 and 2009, the pardoned poultry were shipped off to, you guessed it, Disneyland!

When I first heard this, I was concerned that perhaps the park was running low on one of its favorite concessions, the titanic-sized turkey leg. Thankfully, no. These turkeys really did make it across the country to live in the Happiest Place on Earth as the Happiest Turkeys on Earth. In 2008, President George W. Bush pardoned a forty-five pound bird named Pumpkin. Pumpkin even served as Grand Marshall for that year's Disneyland Thanksgiving Day Parade!

Imagine for just a moment being the Grand Marshall in the parade that celebrates your success. The good news is that you don't have to be a turkey or even need a Presidential Pardon for this to happen. All it takes is gratitude, and a little forced perspective.

DETAILING YOUR DESTINY

*"People will visit this attraction again and again.
Each time, they'll see things they never noticed before."*

DISNEYLAND'S DETAILS

DISNEYLAND IS ALL ABOUT THE details. In fact, so many different details exist that it can be difficult to separate fact from fantasy. The immersion begins the moment you make your way onto Main Street in the morning. If you find yourself a bit hungry, even after a big breakfast, it is not your imagination; vanilla wafts from the vents over the Candy Palace to arouse our appetite. Across the way, in what is now found on every street corner in America, including Disneyland's Main Street, the local Starbucks has a turn-of-the-century telephone. Go ahead; pick up the handset: you can listen in on an old-fashioned party line conversation.

As you make your way to the iconic Sleeping Beauty Castle, you should know that the drawbridge is real and functioning. Disneyland has used it twice: once on opening day in 1955 and again in 1983 with the reopening of Fantasyland, following an extensive remodel. Before deciding which land you would like to explore first, via the spokes of the central hub, pay attention to the Disney Family Crest just above the drawbridge. Walt's family roots reach as far back as the Norman conquest of England in 1066; Hughes D'Isigny fought as a knight during the Battle of Hastings and later settled in Ireland. (Walt's great-grandfather would eventually emigrate to Canada, where his father was born in Ontario in 1859.)

Our quick tour continues on to Adventureland. Here, at the Indiana Jones attraction, the props that provide detail throughout the queue are actual props from the original 1981 movie. In New Orleans Square, we stop to take in the sound coming from the telegraph office at the Disneyland Railroad station. This nineteenth century form of Frontierland communication is sending out a real message: the first two sentences from Walt's opening day dedication:

"To all who come to this happy place, welcome.
Disneyland is your land."

Speaking of Frontierland, be sure to stop along the Rivers of America and take a moment to touch what is easily the oldest attraction in the park, the 55-70 million-year-old petrified tree stump. Walt first found this in Colorado in 1956, and he decided to pick it up as gift for his wife, Lillian. Their wedding anniversary, July 13, was two days away and Walt thought the tree was perfect. Lillian hid her horror for it by telling Walt it was "too large for the mantle at home." She presented it to Disneyland a year later, and it has stood in Frontierland ever since. (I once told this story to a woman with the married last name of Stumpf; even she was stumped by Walt's thinking.)

Near the petrified tree is the Mexican restaurant, Rancho Del Zocala. Originally, this dining facility was named Casa de Fritos and was sponsored by the snack chip giant, Frito-Lay. The next time you are enjoying a bag of Doritos, know that you are also biting into a bit of Disneyland history. Doritos were invented here, in Disneyland, in the 1960s. Originally, they were a byproduct of excess tortillas that the restaurant cut up, fried, and seasoned. They became so popular with park guests that Frito-Lay decided to take Doritos nationwide in

1966. Thus, America's first national tortilla chip was born. The NFL also played its first Super Bowl in 1966. Can you imagine a Super Bowl without Doritos? Now you know you have Disneyland to thank for your favorite snack!

In Fantasyland, you don't want to miss the vastly underrated and underappreciated Storybook Land Canal Boats. All of the miniature houses have six-inch doors with working quarter-inch hinges. Why? So maintenance crews can change the interior lightbulbs, of course! Lastly, take a close look at the "agrifuture" landscaping in Tomorrowland. Everything is edible, which promotes the prospect of a sustainable future and Walt's optimism for our "Great, Big, Beautiful Tomorrow."

Be sure to stop at the end of Main Street before you exit the park at the conclusion of your evening. Walt spent many nights in an apartment above the Main Street Fire Station. After working in the park all night before opening day, Walt slept there for a few hours on the morning of the festivities. Paint was still drying and his door stuck, nearly impeding him from making it to the ceremony just below in Town Square. I invite you to step into the station and touch the fire pole Walt was fond of sliding down first thing in the morning. Walt never lost his youthful enthusiasm, he was just as excited to enter Disneyland as any child visiting for the very first time. Today, a cast member enters the apartment each evening and lights the lamp in the window—a magical reminder that Walt's spirit remains forever in the Kingdom he constructed.

Often at Disneyland, it is difficult to distinguish between what is real and what is make-believe. Once, while riding the *Mark Twain* Riverboat around the Rivers of America, our daughter's boyfriend became very animated. He waved and pointed at something on Tom Sawyer Island that he believed none of us had ever noticed before—an animatronic cat! Although I know the park is populated with hundreds of animatronics, including cats, I also know that Disneyland is home to around 200 feral cats. We were forced to ride the *Mark Twain* Riverboat three times, each time finding the cat in a different location, before convincing the kid that this cat was *real*. (Niki has a favorite feral friend who lives at the park, a fellow she affectionately named Pumpkin Butter.)

Since Disneyland was so personal to Walt, he was hands-on over even the smallest detail. Walt's preference for perfection was reflected in the very first completed attraction at the park, the Disneyland Stage Lines. According to Sam Gennawey in *The Disneyland Story*, John Hench, one of the men who helped Walt build his dream, recalls a conversation he had with Walt when the studio was fabricating the stagecoaches. Hench asked, "Why don't we just leave the leather straps off, Walt? The people are never going to appreciate all this close-up detail." Walt's response to Hench came to be reflected in every attraction that followed: "You're being a poor communicator. People are okay, don't you ever forget that. They will respond to it. They will appreciate it." As a result, Hench and his team (Henchmen, I presume?) ended up putting "the best darned leather straps on that stagecoach you've ever seen."

Art Linkletter, host of Disneyland's opening day broadcast, was fond of telling the story of when he met Walt Disney for the first time, recounted in Williams and Denney's *How to Be Like Walt*. Working in San Francisco, Art was a young broadcaster in 1940 when a local radio station sent him to cover an event where Walt was introducing his latest motion picture, the famed *Fantasia*:

> I arrived early for the press conference, and found the place empty except for one fellow who was busily arranging chairs.
>
> I said, "When is Walt Disney supposed to arrive?" He grinned and said, "I'm Walt Disney."
>
> I said, "You are? Why are you arranging chairs?"
>
> "Well," he said, "I like to have things just-so."

Walt was well-known for being a stickler for details. He very much liked to have things "just-so."

What are the details of your dream? Do you, like Walt, have a hands-on approach to your destiny? Can you define your success as "just-so," or are you merely meandering through life, hoping the magic finds you, and living just "so-so?"

Visualization, your ability to see your dreams coming true down to the tiniest detail in compelling and vivid pictures, is a success principle supported by science, psychiatrists, and even sports coaches. When you provide your brain with as much detail as possible, you are setting your subconscious to work to aid in your success. Your creative subconscious cannot think in words, only pictures. As Jack Canfield says in *The Success Principles,* "If you give your mind a $10,000 problem, it will come up with a $10,000 solution. If you give your mind a $1 million problem, it will come up with a $1 million solution." Walt Disney's dream of Disneyland came with an original price tag of $17 million. His successful solution was to envision the most beautiful, themed, and *detailed* amusement park the world had ever seen.

HICCUPPING YOUR WAY TO SUCCESS

GOING THROUGH BRAIN SURGERY WASN'T the worst part of having a brain tumor. When I awoke from surgery, I actually felt "okay." I wasn't ready to run the Tinker Bell Half Marathon or anything, but I at least knew it was finally over. Neurologically, I knew who I was and where I was.

And then the *real* fun began.

To keep my head from swelling, the neurosurgeon ordered a prescription steroid. He obviously forgot I am an academician with a Ph.D. who works in higher education, so my head swells naturally. Nonetheless, I started swallowing the steroids within an hour of coming out of recovery. Twenty-four hours later, the hiccups started, and over time, they grew progressively more intense and severe. Right before the hospital discharged me, I asked a nurse about my habitual hiccups. She said they were a natural side effect to the steroid so I need not worry.

I hiccupped all the way home.

I hiccupped throughout that first night on my own. I hiccupped through my first full day at home.

Concerned, Niki called the hospital. They advised her to cut the steroid in half, hoping that reducing the dose would resolve the matter. Cutting the dose succeeded. It succeeded in doubling the frequency and intensity of my severe hiccups.

Four days after surviving brain surgery, I feared I was dying from the hiccups. Physically exhausted, I no longer possessed the energy to control my physical responses to the convulsions that consumed me. When breathing on my own became too difficult, I alerted Niki and she rushed me to a local emergency room.

Trauma centers see a variety of survival scenarios each and every day, but the staff are not prepared, apparently, to deal with brain surgery patients who are four days removed from a craniotomy. Aside from giving me oxygen and an IV, the staff was unwilling to treat me without first consulting with my neurosurgeon, who was eighty miles away and mysteriously unavailable.

Eight hours later, the staff finally concocted a series of medications they believed would put me out of my misery. As the nurse was preparing to insert the first injection, I asked him if he thought the medicine would work. His response was less than reassuring. "I don't know. I've never used this drug before. I guess we will find out together!"

Too many of us leave our lives and our success to chance. We survive rather than thrive and "guess" that success will "find" us one day. This way may work for lottery winners, but for the rest of us, it takes a more diligent and detailed approach. You cannot hope to hiccup your way to success.

Visualization is a much better prescription.

ATTRACTING THE IMPOSSIBLE

THE BIGGEST (AND BEST) DREAM I have ever realized is marrying Niki. (Like Walt and Lilly, Niki and I met while working together.) My first marriage ended in failure. After that, I was a pudgy professor who was bald, middle-aged, and muddling through the misery that is a mid-life crisis. I knew Niki would never even notice me; the prospect of her having feelings rested in the realm of the impossible. Since love is always more about fantasy than reality, I began to envision what a life with her would look like. It was a safe dream because I knew Niki lived in Neverland, the land of *never* going to happen!

On a fateful day in February, Niki asked me whether we could talk. Out of the blue, she confessed her feelings for me. I'm not sure who was more shocked—her, learning that we shared mutual feelings, or me, experiencing what it is like to be a dog chasing a car. What do you do when you actually catch it? Soon enough, Niki returned to reality and declared, "It would never work." When I asked her why, she stated, "We come from different worlds." I asked her to keep an open mind and savored the sensation of knowing the hardest part was already done. The impossible had become a possibility. Now it was just a question of details.

One week later, we returned to our original conversation. Niki repeated her previous proclamation that, "It would never work." I replied by agreeing with her that we really did come from different worlds. I also told her it could work, and then, I took it a bit further... not only could it work, but I believed it *would* work. When she asked what I meant, I told her she wasn't ready for what I already knew. Her curiosity piqued, she demanded I explain myself. I repeated that she wasn't ready. Angry, she insisted that I reveal my "inside" information. I then began to vision-cast the life that we now share together....

I began by announcing that we were getting married. This wasn't yet a proposal but instead a revelation. Taking the dream a bit further, I detailed for her where in Arizona the ceremony would take place, a hillside in Sonoita, just outside of Tucson. I would be wearing a taupe suit, a white shirt, and a striped tie. She would be wearing a brown dress, white top, and pearls. I even included the name of the person who would officiate. Lastly, I promised to take her to Hawaii for our honeymoon. Although I'm not much of a romantic, love can give you the ability to leap beyond your limits, and I was proud of the picture I placed before her.

"You are out of your mind!" she yelled. "How can you possibly 'know' this?"

I told her I had seen it. This was my vision and my version of how "us" ended. I reminded her that I had warned her in advance that she wasn't ready to know what I already knew.

She then reiterated, with emphasis, "*You are out of your mind.*" Today, every time we climb the stairs in our home, we see an oversized attraction style poster from our wedding day. The picture is taken from the spot in Sonoita where I originally envisioned the setting for our ceremony many months in advance. Niki is wearing a brown dress, white top, and pearls. I am wearing a taupe suit, white shirt, and striped tie. Even the minister was the clergy member I forecasted. Granted, his last name was Smith (the most popular name in the United States), so I might have gotten lucky on that one. But still, I think you see my point.

I only missed one detail. By the time we were married, we already knew we were moving to Hawaii in a few short months. So where did we go instead? You guessed it:

"Jeff, you just married the woman of your dreams!
What are you going to do next?"

"We're going to Disneyland!"

SOUVENIR STOP

Let's borrow an exercise from Jack Canfield and other success coaches. Take a moment to visualize your dream. Effective visualization is more than just "seeing" success. It involves evoking ALL of your senses. If you want to possess the ever elusive "sixth sense of success," you must first begin by using the five senses God has already blessed you with.

Remember our quick tour of Disneyland? Did you notice how our stops along the way combined a collection of sensory experiences? For example:

1. **Sight:** Castle Drawbridge, Disney Family Crest, Indiana Jones Props, House Hinges in Storybook Land, and Walt Disney's Apartment Lamp
2. **Sound:** Turn-of-the-Century Telephone and Train Station Telegraph
3. **Smell**: Vanilla Scent from Candy Palace Confections
4. **Taste**: Disneyland Doritos and Tomorrowland's Edible Agrifuture
5. **Touch**: Lillian's Petrified Tree and Walt's Firehouse Pole

"The fact is, as we stand here right now [in Disneyland], there are literally hundreds of stimuli etching an impression and an experience in our minds through every one of our senses."

— John Hench

Now, let's say your dream is to own a nicer home. Close your eyes and imagine yourself walking through the exact house of your dreams. Include as much detail as possible. For example:

1. **Sight**: What color is the exterior? What kind of view does it have? What types of pictures, paintings, and furniture accentuate each room? Again, be exact in every detail with *images* that are as clear and bright as possible.
2. **Sound**: Are you in the country where it is quiet and peaceful? Or perhaps your dream is a penthouse in downtown Manhattan. Either way, take time to *hear* the vision that is your new home.

3. **Smell**: Yes, your dream has an aromatic attribute as well. Can you *smell* your favorite dish cooking in the kitchen? Go ahead and envision walking into your brand new home with the smell of fresh paint and new floors. I bet your dream smells great, doesn't it?
4. **Taste**: Speaking of taste, imagine for a moment sitting down in your new kitchen and eating your favorite meal. Does this image make you hungry? Good! Successful people keep themselves hungry... hungry enough to pursue their dreams relentlessly and without fail.
5. **Touch:** Take one last detailed tour of your new home. This time, *touch* each of the furnishings. *Feel* the wood of your coffee table and the upholstery of your living room couch. Linger over your fine linens and know that your subconscious is going to work to help make your dream a definite reality.

Regardless of your actual dream, be it to own a nicer home, have a more challenging career, lose weight, or write that book, know that you can do it and that visualization can help get you there. Go ahead; be a person with embarrassingly big goals, knowing you can produce impressive results. With visualization, you can already see how your story ends.

> *"Everyone of our senses are coming into play....This is total involvement. You can never capture this moment and take it home with you in a camera or tape recorder. You can only take this experience home in your mind."*
>
> —John Hench

GETTING YOUR HAND STAMPED

I WANT TO SHARE ONE more Art Linkletter story. This one is from Anaheim. One day, Walt invited Art to drive down with him from Los Angeles to see where he was building Disneyland. Interested in the details of Walt's dream, Art readily agreed. It was 1954, so there was still not much to see other than some bulldozers, a cleared out orange grove, and a big dirt field. The story is recounted in Williams and Denney's *How to Be Like Walt* in Linkletter's own words:

> Well, Walt said, "This is it." He looked around and he could see it all in his imagination: the Disneyland Railroad, Main Street, Sleeping Beauty Castle, Adventureland, Frontierland, Fantasyland, Tomorrowland. I looked around and saw nothing but a cow pasture. I thought, *My poor deluded friend! He's going to put a bunch of merry-go-rounds and roller-coasters out here, forty-five minutes from L.A. He'll go broke!*

Albert Einstein once said, "Imagination is everything. It is the preview of life's coming attractions." Know that your dreams are indeed possible. You just need to evoke the emotions of all your senses. Your success, your dreams, your destiny rest in the details of your imagination.

KEEPING FANTASY AT THE HEART OF EVERYTHING

"Fantasy and reality often overlap."

DISNEYLAND'S TRUE NORTH

NOT ALL LANDS IN DISNEYLAND are created equal. From the beginning, Walt intended for each locale to evoke a certain sense of place and serve a particular purpose. Main Street harkens back to turn-of-the-century America when we were technologically torn between the gas lamp and the electric lamp, the horse and the horse-less carriage. Adventureland serves as a reminder of exotic people and places that span the faraway places of our planet. Frontierland is an homage to the hard-working, risk-taking people of the past who settled America and made us who we are today. Tomorrowland celebrates the possibilities of the future and envisions an always better tomorrow.

Walt introduced his radical idea for a new form of entertainment, the theme park, to a national audience, via his television show, *Disneyland*, on October 27, 1954. In this ABC broadcast, he talks about how the park's lands branch out from the Central Hub, just past Main Street, like the four cardinal points of the compass. The final land, Fantasyland, "the Happiest Land of Them All," lies to the North. The gateway into Fantasyland is Sleeping Beauty Castle, today recognized worldwide as *the* symbol for all of Disneyland. After all, as Walt himself said, "A castle is fantasy in any language."

Anyone who has ever visited Disneyland is sure to have felt the castle's power to transport you into a world of fantasy. As John Hench said, "If you walked up and asked a guest WHY he likes the castle, WHY it is worth photographing? He could never tell you. He'd probably stammer out something like, 'Because it's just beautiful.' And yet, when he gets back home and shows his pictures, the feeling will never be the same that he experiences simply standing there."

For many, Walt's idea of Disneyland was just that—fantasy; a figment of Walt's ever wild imagination and so impossible and improbable that few believed it would ever come to fruition. On opening day, when Walt's fantasy finally became reality, he dedicated each new land in Disneyland. Here are his words for Fantasyland:

> Here is a land of imagination, hopes and dreams. In this timeless land of enchantment the age of chivalry, magic and make-believe are reborn and fairy tales come true. Fantasyland is dedicated to the young and the young at heart, to those who believe that when you wish upon a star your dreams do come true.

Fantasyland isn't just north in Disneyland; it represents Walt Disney's "True North." Walt lived his life believing that fantasy and fun should be at the heart of everything we do. Imagination isn't just for kids, and fantasy isn't just a land in a theme park. Walt once said, "That's the real trouble with the world, too many people grow up."

Walt loved Fantasyland. It was clearly his favorite place in the park, and he considered it to be the very heart of Disneyland. It has always hosted the most number of attractions, nineteen as of this writing, versus, say, four in today's Adventureland. When you love what you are doing, and you are having fun doing it, then you are living out your own form of Fantasyland. Your fantasy becomes your truth. You are on course with your own "True North."

I've already shared with you the fantasy life I am living with my wife, Niki. I now want to invite you onto an "attraction," a story from one of our earliest escapades. Here we find ourselves in France, Niki's lifelong fantasy destination. What follows is a fun retelling of one of our greatest adventures. This story, "Sans Flash," is a reflection of my love for her and my desire to keep the love of my life at the center of everything.

Like most attractions in Fantasyland, this stand-alone story does not have a height requirement. But please keep your arms and legs inside at all times. No flash photography. Oh, and be sure to watch your children!

Sans Flash

A FEW YEARS AGO, WHILE living in Hawaii, Niki and I decided to celebrate Christmas in Paris. Before we could take off, we first had to visit the local library. You see, Niki is a master planner and a rabid researcher, but not me. I avoid libraries like an overdue book. This time, she was insistent. "We have books to browse, periodicals to peruse, maps to memorize, and language lessons to learn!"

"Whoa! Stop the Metro! Language lessons? What language?" Apparently, Paris is in France, and the French prefer to speak, well, French. My friends often accuse me of speaking English as if it were my own foreign tongue, so French was now the official language in the Land of Never Going to Happen.

Each day, Niki added voluminously to her vocabulary. Meanwhile, I did what I always do. I procrastinated. *Surely,* I thought, *she's learning enough French for the both of us.* By the time we left Hawaii, Niki possessed a Rosetta Stone's repertoire of French words and phrases. Personally, I prefer to pack a little lighter.

I landed in Paris with all of two words.

My first French word was "sans." Sans means "no" or "without." Sans allowed me to parade through the streets of Paris repeating over and over again, "Sans French. Sans French," then turn all transactions over to my beautiful, charming, and fanatically prepared wife.

My second word was "Merci," meaning "Thank you." Like "sans," it is a good, safe, and purposeful word. I believe in expressing gratitude. I believe it is important to say "Thank you" as often as possible. The challenge is that when I say "Merci," I end up pronouncing it "mercy." Translation? Every conversation I attempted ended with "Have mercy on me; I speak no French."

Paris is famous for the Eiffel Tower, the Louvre, the Arc de Triomphe, and a host of other world-class tourist attractions. But guess where we went first?

Disneyland!

We soon stood on Main Street, U.S.A., in the middle of France, simultaneously comforted and disconcerted. How could something so similar also feel so strange?

The first answer is weather. Disney has proven that you can mass produce Magic Kingdoms in multiple locations. Each comes complete with its own castle, mountain range, flying elephant, etc. What you cannot export from the authentic Anaheim original, however, is climate.

We shivered at sunrise that December day in below-freezing temperatures. Our senses took in the traffic that fills Main Street each morning. We saw the horses. We saw the omnibuses. We saw the fire wagons.

Then we spotted it.

A snowplow?

Niki and I snuggled in a little closer. Two Hawaiian Eskimos lost in a fantasyland of the familiar.

The weather in Paris is different. So are the people. As we walked toward the castle, we found ourselves enveloped by a cosmopolitan collection of cultures and countries. At Disneyland in California, people come primarily from different states. In Europe, they come from different *continents.*

The day divided itself between a war to stay warm and endless exposure to the warm people of the world who packed the park. We experienced every available attraction, and by the end of the evening, we found ourselves right back at the beginning—on Main Street, U.S.A.

Niki and I paused for one last parting picture. We reversed our camera and attempted to snap a shot of ourselves with the castle (Le Château de la Belle au Bois Dormant) illuminated in the background. We fought to get the angle just right, to no avail. Eventually, an Asian family took pity on us and the father offered to assist. I guided him through the camera's controls, and then Niki and I stood in place for the perfect picture.

That's when I remembered.

That's when my preparation paid off.

That's when my research reaped its rewards.

In planning for the trip, I did manage to read a quick tip article on how to take better photographs. One short suggestion said to turn the flash off when attempting a picture at night in a well-lit environment, e.g., Main Street, U.S.A.

"Sans flash!" I yelled. "Sans flash!"

The man, knowing neither French nor English, snapped the shot. Frustrated, I began screaming, in my most awesome Asian accent, "Sans flash! Sans Flash!"

The frightened faces on Main Street all possessed the same quizzical look. Who is this guy? When did *loud* become an international language?

Niki, convinced more than ever that I must have grown up with deaf people, quieted me with a hush. "The problem, dear, isn't that he can't hear you. The problem is he doesn't understand you."

I like to live life loud. Words.

Stories. Noise.

Us simpletons who are "sans understanding" simply pump up the volume and expect the people dialed in around us to adjust. We all need that special someone who understands us better than we could ever understand ourselves. A friend who is fearless with perspective. A partner whose heartbeat is so loud it deafens the noise of our own narcissism.

Love is the most difficult language of all. Over the years, Niki has taught me a few words and a couple of phrases. Every now and then, I even get the pronunciation right.

"Merci, Niki." "Merci."

SOUVENIR STOP

WOW. JUST LIKE AT DISNEYLAND, when you exit a ride or attraction, now as you exit my story, you find yourself in our little souvenir shop. While we are here, let's explore some questions that can help you keep fantasy at the heart of everything.

ARE YOU HAVING FUN? I really don't think we ask this question nearly enough. Somewhere between the carefree world of childhood and the responsibilities of being an adult, we let go of our fantasies, our imaginations, our hopes, our dreams, and our world of make-believe. We think having fun, especially when it comes to work, is the stuff of fairy tales. Responsibility means taking life seriously, which equals no more fun.

Why?

I believe we are at our best when we are having fun. Today, the Disney Corporation is one of the most valued companies in the world, and it was created by a man who found a way to have fun in everything he did. I guess it is a good thing Walt Disney never took himself too seriously!

Why should you?

"Every child is blessed with a vivid imagination.
But just as a muscle grows flabby with disuse,
so the bright imagination of a child pales in later
years if he ceases to exercise it."

— Walt Disney

Do You Love It? In the past few years, I have been to Disneyland well over 150 times. Why? Because I love it. What else do you need to know?

Love is rooted in fantasy, meaning there is no rational explanation. What did Niki ever see in me? I have no idea. I just know that I am much happier going along for the ride with her than stopping to ask unnecessary questions. We love what we love. The only real question is whether or not we love ourselves enough to go after our dreams and live the life we are always fantasizing about. Or as author Jen Sincero puts it:

> But what if you had the audacity to leave your excuses and your shame about wanting to be huge and fabulous behind and really went for it full-on anyway? What if you decided to do the most outrageous, most exciting thing you ever dared fantasize about, regardless of what anyone, including your terrified self, thought? THAT would be living.

Does It Keep You Young? Or at Least Young at Heart? During my first visit to a Disney playground in 1971, one of the attractions I most looked forward to riding was Dumbo the Flying Elephant. I had so much fun on my ninety-second journey that I spent my small souvenir allowance purchasing a stuffed Dumbo to take home. The first time I went with my daughter Bethany to Disneyland, she was three. I insisted that we ride Dumbo, first—together. She is all grown now, but we still ride it together whenever we can. Riding Dumbo may not be typical behavior for investigative journalists, college deans, or university professors. It is, however, for the young and the young at heart. Why not give it a spin?

"Why do we have to grow up?"

— Walt Disney

GETTING YOUR HAND STAMPED

FOUR DAYS BEFORE DISNEYLAND OPENED, July 13, 1955, Walt and Lillian celebrated their thirtieth wedding anniversary. They invited guests to join them for a "Tempus Fugit" (time flies) celebration at the not-yet-finished park. Their friends began arriving at 6 p.m. and were driven down Main Street, U.S.A. in horse-drawn surreys to Frontierland and the *Mark Twain* Riverboat, for its maiden voyage around the Rivers of America. They sipped mint juleps on their journey and then walked over to the Golden Horseshoe Saloon. There, dinner was served and Wally Boag gave the first of 47,250 performances as Pecos Bill in the Golden Horseshoe Revue.

This thirtieth anniversary represents the perfect marriage of love (Walt and Lillian), Fantasy (Disneyland), Fun (*Mark Twain* Riverboat and the Golden Horseshoe Revue), and Friendship (all those who gathered for the celebration). Some who were there believe it was the happiest night of Walt Disney's incredible life.

Williams and Denney recount in *How to Be Like Walt* that when the party was finally over, Walt was hesitant to go home, "...he stood there beaming at everyone. He was so happy." Eventually, the family exited the park. According to Walt's daughter, Diane:

> Dad just climbed in the back seat of the car.... He had a map of Disneyland, and he rolled it up and tooted in my ear as if with a toy trumpet. He sang for a while—then, before I knew it, everything was silent in the back seat. I looked around and there he was, his arms folded around the map like a boy with a toy trumpet, sound asleep.

The lesson? Love who you are with. Have fun in everything you do. Keep fantasy at the heart of everything.

"Our fantasies are the most revealing peepholes
into who we are and what we think is awesome.
No matter how out-there and ridiculous they may seem,
they mean something to us, and usually represent our
biggest and best versions of ourselves."

— Jen Sincero

TAKING CARE OF YOUR TEAM

"You can design and create and build the most wonderful place in the world. But it takes people to make the dream a reality."

WHAT'S IN A NAME?

IT MAY NOT SEEM LIKE much, but one small detail in Disneyland sheds light on Walt's leadership and vision. Pay attention; it is important, so you won't want to miss it. Look at the name badge of the first cast member you come across. Do you see what it says? It only includes the employee's first name and his or her hometown. What the badge *doesn't* say speaks volumes about Walt and Disneyland.

Walt Disney always insisted on only ever being referred to as "Walt." Longtime team members knew that he hated it when anyone called him "Mr. Disney." In *The Revised Vault of Walt*, Jim Korkis retells a story from Renie Bardeau, who for years worked as Disneyland's official photographer. Bardeau was sitting on Main Street, U.S.A. one morning, well before the park's opening, drinking coffee and reading a newspaper. Walt stopped by and asked whether he could join him. A waitress came to take Walt's order and was physically shaking as she asked, "Mr. Disney," what he wanted. Bardeau has never forgotten Walt's response: "There are only two misters in Disneyland. Mr. Lincoln and Mr. Toad. Call me Walt."

"Call me Walt." Picture this for just a moment. Walt Disney owned both the studio and park that bore his name. He knew that if being called by his first name was good enough for him, then it was good enough for everyone else, too. According to Van Arsdale France in *Window on Main Street,* this is how Walt built his team. "Walt insisted that people call each other, and him, by their first names.... Walt didn't like pretentions, status-seeking, title-happy people or stuffed shirts. He either put them down or got rid of them."

Walt understood well an often-overlooked secret to success and leadership. No one person can do it alone. You need your team, and teams are best built around a common, shared interest or goal rather than from positions of power or authority. In Walt's own words, "Only through the talent, the labor and the dedication of the staff could any Disney project get off the ground." Walt Disney left a lengthy legacy, but his team building may well be his most lasting. Regarding his success, Walt once said with pride that, "Of all the things I've done, the most vital is coordinating those who work with me and aiming their efforts at a certain goal."

Walt Disney couldn't do it alone, and neither can you or I. Let's explore how Walt built his teams. The lessons here are transferable. Regardless of whether Walt was making cartoons, leading a studio, or building theme parks, his team-building principles remained the same. Anyone can learn these lessons, apply these principles, and achieve the same results with his or her team that Walt achieved.

PUTTING THE "US" IN TRUST

WALT DISNEY TRUSTED HIS TEAM. At Disneyland, he trusted his team to put on a first-class show. He didn't hire employees but rather "cast members." Regardless of position, be it janitor, baker, attraction lead, or vice-president, each cast member is personally responsible for that day's performance and ensuring an outstanding guest experience. Walt had high expectations about guest service, and he expected each cast member to exceed those expectations long before a guest actually entered the gates of Disneyland.

According to Sam Gennawey in *The Disneyland Story*, "Walt knew that first impressions mattered, and one of the greatest sensitivity points in the entire Disneyland experience was the parking lot.... As guests drove into the parking lot, they would be guided to one of the 12,175 empty parking stalls by uniformed parking attendants acting more like ushers."

Walt wanted his cast members to have as many interactions with guests as possible, even his "ushers" or parking lot attendants. Walt ensured that they were trained to be passionate ambassadors for his Magic Kingdom and were committed to its key concepts. Once inside the park, guests needed an individual ticket or coupon for each attraction. One of the reasons why Walt valued the ticket booths and the ticket books they sold is because they ensured extra opportunities for cast members to interact with guests and "plus" or enhance their experience throughout the day.

Can you imagine such an idea in today's world of automation? Unfortunately, it appears that the goal of many leaders and their companies is to keep employees as far away from customers as possible. While there are many reasons for this distance, I want to challenge you with this question: Do you *really* trust your team members? If you do, then like Walt, shouldn't your goal be for them to have *more* interactions with your customers, not less?

As explained by Bill Capodagli and Lynn Jackson in *The Disney Way*, Disneyland's stellar reputation for phenomenal customer service was built on Walt's belief that in the mind of the customer, every employee was the company. If you can't trust your employees with your company, then how can you possibly trust them with your customers?

"He [Walt] built a trust. No challenge ever scared you because of that trust."

— Imagineer Bob Gurr

ALL ABOARD!

THE DISNEYLAND RAILROAD ISN'T THE only train at Walt's Magic Kingdom. Getting people moving in the same direction takes *train*ing. The "us" in trust isn't just about hiring the right people but also ensuring that each new team member is also properly trained. Before Disneyland ever opened, Walt hired Van Arsdale France to develop an orientation program for prospective cast members. Van had extensive experience in developing training programs for aircraft corporations. Nothing like Disneyland existed, however, so he had to create everything from scratch. In *Window on Main Street*, France recalls, "...here I was developing a program for people operating a crazy dream." Note that Walt didn't micro-manage his own orientation program. "We had one policy direct from Walt," continues France. "He hated the dirt and sloppy service he got elsewhere."

What is most significant about France's program isn't that he trained cast members on "how" to do their jobs. Instead, he focused more on "why" their jobs existed. There is an often-told story about two men in the Middle Ages who are busy laying bricks. One is obviously miserable, and when asked what he is doing, his response is, "I'm laying bricks." In stark contrast, the other man is excited, animated, and filled with joy as he goes about his business. He, too, is asked what he is doing. "I'm building a cathedral!"

France wanted cathedral builders, or at least castle builders, not bricklayers. He built his training program around the idea of "creating happiness." Regardless of person or position, specific job skills or competencies, every cast member was challenged to get aboard the same train going to the same station. Here are Walt's words from the opening page of the original orientation program:

Welcome to Disneyland.

To make the dream of Disneyland come true took the combined skills and talents of artisans, carpenters,

> *engineers, scientists and planners. The dream they built now becomes your heritage. It is you who will make Disneyland truly a magic kingdom and a happy place for the millions of guests who will visit us now and in future years. In creating happiness for our guests, I hope that you will find happiness in your work and in being an important part of Disneyland.*

Disneyland's original training program has evolved into what we know today as "Disney University." Now this is a university where I would love to be the dean! The campus consists of all the acres at both Disneyland and Walt Disney World, and anywhere else the company operates. It focuses on the pivotal process of training and retraining Disney employees, including theme park cast members, on the cultures and traditions unique to Disney. These cultures and traditions, of course, started with Walt himself.

Once the hiring and training is done, then you, as a leader, only have one job left. You must let these individuals go and allow them to serve you, your company, and your customers. Per Walt, "As well as I can I'm untying the apron strings—until they scream for help."

Taking care of your team also means making sure you hold on to the right team members. Because of his vision and how he treated his team, Walt had no problem holding on to those who served him well. Walt himself once recounted that, "No matter what the provocation, I never fire a man who is honestly trying to deliver a job. Few workers who become established at the Disney Studio ever leave voluntarily or otherwise, and many have been on the payroll all their working lives."

Know, however, that Walt worked both ways. Sometimes, taking care of your team also means letting go of team members who aren't working. Or at least those who don't "get" the vision. In *Walt Disney: An American Original,* Bob Thomas shares the following story about a rare Walt Disney firing:

> One evening Walt and Lilly were stopped by a guard while approaching a preview of the Monsanto exhibit. When Walt explained who he was, the guard said, "All right, you can go in, but she can't." Walt later ordered the guard fired, saying, "If he treats me that way, imagine how he'll be with other people."

Walt always wanted the best for his employees, but he also knew the customers came first; otherwise, there would be no jobs for the employees.

"We train them to be aware that they're there mainly to help the guests."

— Walt Disney

ALOHA

AFTER NINE YEARS OF SUCCESS in Arizona, I was asked by the university whether I would be willing to transfer to Hawaii. The campus there had struggled for years, and administration believed the leadership principles I employed in Arizona could also turn the ship around in Hawaii.

My first day on the job was mass confusion. I knew there would be a transition period from my years in Arizona to a new team of people in Hawaii that knew nothing about me. If nothing else, day one convinced me that I was underestimating the transition I was facing.

The campus facility was located in a strip mall. It was a hodgepodge collection of classrooms, corridors, and confusion. Regardless of where I turned, I was constantly locked out once the door behind me closed. Frustrated, I found our assistant dean and asked what was up with all of the locks and keys. He explained to me that the previous dean was fastidious about security and cost control. If an employee needed a Post-it note, she had to ask the dean for it, and he would procure the pad from a locked cabinet. Ditto any other office supply, including toilet paper. I asked whether these constraints had been financially successful. Of course, I already knew the answer; year after year, the Hawaii campus had been running in the red.

I ushered every other team member into my office and held up a loaded ring of keys. I then gave my first order. By the end of the week, I wanted the campus reduced to a single key, the one necessary for locking and unlocking the front door. They were to unlock everything else and keep it all open. After an audible gasp, I provided them with perspective: "Every time the phone rings or someone walks through the front door, you are dealing with a potential $30,000-plus customer. If I can trust you with that transaction, and I do, then I am fairly certain I can also trust you with a Post-it note or a roll of toilet paper."

This initial conversation set the tone for my tenure. Morale soared, and I am proud to say that less than eighteen months later, the budget deficit the campus had endured for years became a thing of the past. Fortunately, I had inherited a terrific team, and each member of it knew how to do his or her job. My task was to train all of them on creating a culture of trust.

"I don't pose as an authority on anything at all,
I follow the opinions of the ordinary people I meet,
and I take pride in the close-knit teamwork
with my organization."

— Walt Disney

SOUVENIR STOP

When it comes to success, everyone is looking for a shortcut. The same is true when it comes to tips for taking care of your team. I want to share with you a simple strategy that has worked for me in my many years of leadership and team building. It isn't difficult. It's not expensive.

Everyone can do it. I am not aware of a quicker way to build trust and rapport with your team than what I am about to share with you.

Are you ready? Good!

Here goes...

WRITE PERSONAL THANK YOU NOTES.

I suspect I know what you are already thinking. We live in the era of electronics. We live in the age of technology. Writing thank you notes, especially handwriting them, is obsolete. Nobody does it. If I have to be thankful, why can't I just send a text or a tweet to that valued team member? I can always Like a post on Facebook or, if I need to exhibit some level of effort, fire off a computer-generated letter. You aren't wrong. Nobody sends handwritten thank you notes anymore.

And that is *exactly* my point.

When Walt set out to build Disneyland, he traveled the country and parts of the world touring and studying amusement parks. Ever curious, Walt asked operators lots of questions and took copious notes. Whenever he talked about his own ideas with those already in the business, they scoffed at what we know today to be "Walt's Way."

"You aren't going to have a Ferris wheel?"

"What do you mean there is only one way in and one way out, through Main Street, an area with no real rides, shows, or attractions?"

"You are going to spend all that money on landscaping and theming? And you think the public will notice, let alone care?" This last one is my favorite. Walt's desire to make Disneyland as beautiful as possible reflects well the words of Daniel Burnham, famed Chicago architect of the 1893 World's Fair (where Walt's father once worked as a carpenter), "Beauty has always paid better than any other commodity and always will."

Walt already possessed a compelling vision of what he wanted Disneyland to be. He designed Disneyland to be different and distinct from everything else that was already out there. He wasn't studying other operations so he could copy them. Walt was busy learning what *not* to do with Disneyland. He expected to shatter expectations.

Look for every opportunity to take the road less travelled. You need to be different. You need to be distinct. Since no one writes handwritten thank you notes anymore, why not commit to writing at least one, to at least one team member, once per week? The results will be astounding, and your team will never forget you for it. Start now by making a list of those to whom you want to write thank you notes.

1. ______________________________
2. ______________________________
3. ______________________________
4. ______________________________
5. ______________________________

"One of Walt's strengths in his relationship with talent was that he made it clear he cared about us."

— Marty Sklar

GETTING YOUR HAND STAMPED

DISNEYLAND HAS ITS OWN THANK you notes. Like many other areas of the park, Main Street was still incomplete on opening day. According to Sam Gennawey in *The Disneyland Story*, Imagineers, in an effort to hide this fact from guests, hid unfinished storefronts with signs such as, "Harper Goff will be opening his store here soon." Harper Goff was an individual who played an instrumental role in the early development and construction of Disneyland. "This was the start of a long tradition at Disneyland to honor those who have contributed to the park's success," says Gennawey.

Today, there is no higher honor for a Disney employee than to receive a famed "Window on Main Street." In theatrical terms, these thank you notes are a form of opening and closing "credits," recognizing the significant contributions of many different team members over the years who helped make the dream of Disneyland. In case you are curious, here are the three requirements for receiving such an honor:

1. Only on retirement
2. Only the highest level of service/respect/achievement
3. Agreement between top individual park management and Walt Disney Imagineering.

Who are your team members? How are you thanking them and honoring them for the roles they are playing as you achieve your dreams? Taking care of your team, be they friends, family, and/or employees, is a main element on your road to success.

Remember Disneyland's longtime photographer? At the end of Main Street above the Photo Supply Store is a window that reads "Kingdom Photo Services—Renie Bardeau—Photographer, Archivist." You can never be certain, but I believe a man named "Walt" would approve.

Creating E-Ticket Experiences

"Do what you do so well that they will want to see it again and bring their friends."

"E" IS FOR "EXCEEDING EXPECTATIONS"

We rarely remember it, but Disneyland used to have a separate admission for entry into the park and then individual tickets for the various attractions. Today, we are so accustomed to the one-day, multi-day, and annual passport ticket system that few know or remember the original pricing structure. However, the original pay-per-ride system is a fascinating story and offers a wonderful leadership lesson on creating an exceptional customer experience.

When Disneyland opened on July 17, 1955, the general admission price was $1.00. This ticket was only good for entry into the park with individual tickets required for each attraction.

These tickets ranged in price from .10 cents to .35 cents for the original opening day attractions. Walt realized quickly, however, that he needed to develop a system that would both help simplify guests' expenses and enhance their park experience. On October 11, 1955, he introduced the very first Disneyland ticket book. This value package cost each guest $2.50 and included park admission, plus tickets, or "coupons," to eight of the park's twenty-one attractions.

Most memorably, the original ticket book classified attractions into categories "A," "B," and "C." "A" tickets represented minor attractions, "C" tickets were the best experiences the park had to offer, and "B" attractions were somewhere in between.

The original ticket book expanded in 1958 to include "D" coupons. The final update came in 1959 and was simultaneous with the park's first big expansion. By that year, the success of Disneyland was no longer in question. With money on hand and financing now readily available, Walt naturally turned his attention toward Tomorrowland, the area of the park that was constructed last and suffered most from money shortfalls that invariably plagued Walt during construction. Simply stated, Tomorrowland was not up to the standards that Walt had set throughout the remainder of the park. On opening day, many of the Tomorrowland attractions were mere corporate exhibits. The "land" was almost all open space with the little bit of "landscaping" that did exist consisting of weeds that, at the last moment, had been ingeniously labeled in Latin to make them appear intentional until proper landscaping could be done. According to Bob Thomas in *Walt Disney: An American Original*:

> Walt's principal concern was meeting the impossible deadline.... By January 1, 1955, it seemed imperative that some compromises had to be made. Tomorrowland was the least developed section of Disneyland; Walt agreed to his staff's suggestion to board up Tomorrowland with an attractive fence, announcing that it would open later. No sooner was the decision made than Walt rescinded it. "We'll open the whole park," he told his staff. "Do the best you can with Tomorrowland, and we'll fix it up after we open."

All of this changed in 1959. In one fell swoop, Walt transformed Tomorrowland into the "Land of Tomorrow" that he had originally envisioned. This expansion included the addition of three major attractions: the submarine voyage and its famed journey through "liquid space," the monorail, and the first of Disneyland's many mountains, the Matterhorn. Each new attraction represented a major advancement in technology and guest experience, giving birth to the famed Disneyland "E-ticket" for the best attractions the park had to offer. As stated earlier, the ticket books started with A, B, and C coupons; then Ds were included, and lastly Es for the newest or best attractions.

All three of these attractions remain in the park today, and the Matterhorn Bobsleds may well be the most unique. First, it sparked the range of mountains for which all Disney parks are now famous. Secondly, it became an instant symbol for children anywhere in Southern California. Once they could "spot" the Matterhorn Mountain, they knew they had arrived, at last, for their long-anticipated day at Disneyland. Today, the Matterhorn Bobsleds is no longer listed as a Tomorrowland attraction. Instead, it actually lives in Fantasyland. Walt didn't "move mountains," Disneyland just decided one day to redraw the boundaries. It is a reminder, however, as recounted in Gennawey's *The Disneyland Story*, of Joe Fowler's remark to Walt regarding the Matterhorn Bobsleds opening in time for the 1959 celebration. "I think we'll have it finished on time, but next time, when we have to build a mountain, let's let God do it."

In 1983, the first American woman in space, Sally Ride (you can't make this name up), was asked about her space shuttle launch. She famously replied, "Have you ever been to Disneyland? That was definitely an E-ticket!" You know you are doing something right when you receive a nationally televised celebrity endorsement of your product, all the way from outer space, for free!

Have you ever wondered what it takes to get free advertising for your story, your product, or your brand? Have you ever asked yourself what it is about an Apple product that merits its fan base camping out in the elements the night before a major product launch? Perhaps you, too, have willingly turned over your hard-earned money for a $3.00

cup of Starbucks coffee and asked yourself what Starbucks does that allows it to charge such a premium price for what was once a fifty-cent cup of Joe?

The answer is in the experience. And not just *any* experience, but a *memorable*, E-ticket experience!

It seems obvious to us now, sixty years later, but given that everyone believed initially that Walt and Disneyland were destined to fail, one cannot help but wonder how and why it became such a success so quickly. The answer lies in Walt's insatiable desire not only to meet, but also to exceed his guests' expectations. Exceed really is the "E" in every E-ticket experience!

DOING VERSUS HAVING

THE FIRST GIFT I EVER gave Niki was her own little piece of Disneyland. It wasn't much, but I am madly in love with Niki and Disneyland, so connecting the two as quickly as possible filled an obvious need for me. I went online and found a ticket book from 1977, the year she was born. My palms sweated and my heart palpitated as the minutes to the eBay auction ticked down. When at last I won, I saw it as an immediate sign that I would be successful in winning her heart as well.

I couldn't wait to give her the gift. I found a card that safely communicated my feelings toward her without risking too much, and I was confident the ticket book would say the rest. Niki was appreciative, which was more reflective of her nature than her valuing my gift or her recognition of my burgeoning feelings for her. She confessed to me that she didn't really understand the gift because she had never been to Disneyland.

I then proclaimed that if she were interested in knowing anything about me, she also needed to know about Walt Disney and Disneyland. A bit of explanation was in order, so I lectured her on the history of Disneyland's ticketing system and walked her through the different attractions represented on the various A, B, C, D, and E coupons. When she was still lost, I pointed out this wasn't just any old Disneyland ticket book (like there is such a thing!), but one from 1977, the year my favorite attraction, Space Mountain, opened *and* the year she was born. Ohhhhhhh!

The only way she was ever really going to understand was to experience Disneyland herself, an experience I was happy to share with her on our honeymoon the following year. Giving her the ticket book gift was a great gesture, but we valued the experience, together, far more.

Most people do.

We spend far too much time and money chasing material possessions—possessions that bring us little pleasure and often end up possessing us. What we truly crave are experiences and the opportunity to share those experiences with those we love. In his book *The Happiness Hypothesis,* Jonathan Haidt explores recent research regarding "doing versus having." Most people are far happier having spent $100 or more on an experience or activity than a material possession. Why? "Most activities that cost more than a hundred dollars are things we do *with* other people, but expensive material possessions are often purchased in part to *impress* other people. Activities connect us to others; objects often separate us."

"E" IS FOR "EXPERIENCE"

WITHOUT RESEARCH AND YEARS OF twenty-first century data, Walt was already tuned in to the importance of experience. In Sam Gennawey's *The Disneyland Story,* Disney legend John Hench, who worked with Walt in creating the experience that is Disneyland, is quoted as saying:

> Walt was a firm believer in experience. He said that experiences were the only thing that you really own. They were yours. The example he would talk about was with apples.

> He said you could see pictures of apples, but you didn't know what an apple was until you sank your teeth into one. Then it was a matter of experience.

Most significantly, Walt Disney refused to settle. He was often challenged on all sides to eviscerate his vision for the sake of cutting costs or compromising to the demands of others. He held fast. The lessons on customer service and providing a phenomenal guest experience are extensive:

Town Square: Disneyland wouldn't be Disneyland without Main Street, USA with its Town Square sitting at the start. Veteran amusement park operators hated both. Scoffers shouted that the entire scheme was too expensive, unnecessary, and a waste of precious space that would generate virtually zero income. In *Walt Disney: An American Original,* Bob Thomas states, "Walt listened to them and made no change. He intended the Town Square to set the mood for visitors. It would be a place with flowers and balloons, costumes and a brass band. Handsomely wrought surreys, a fire wagon and a horse-drawn trolley would take people down Main Street and to the rest of the realms. The vehicles would not have enough capacity to make a profit, but they contributed to the entire experience."

The Souvenir Guidebook: Like everything else, the cost of producing and printing Disneyland's hallmark souvenir guidebook increased over time. When the price points nearly met, .24 cents to make versus .25 cents in revenue, Walt's merchandising team advocated doubling the price to .50 cents. Walt's answer was "No." According to Marty Sklar in *Dream It! Do It!,* "Walt's reasons were clear and direct. 'Look,' he said, 'we don't have to make a profit on *every* line of merchandise. Our guests take those souvenir books home, put them on their coffee tables, and their friends see them and think, 'That place looks like fun!' And when they come, they buy tickets to the park, and food, and merchandise inside. That's when we'll make our profit. Keep the price at 25 cents; I want as many souvenir books as you can sell in homes across the country—around the world.'"

An Administration Building: Soon enough, the Disneyland management team wanted Walt to build something for them, an administration building. Bob Thomas recounts that Walt resisted with this reasoning, "The public isn't coming here to see an administration building. Besides, I don't want you guys sitting behind desks. I want you out in the park, watching what people are doing and finding out how you can make the place more enjoyable for them."

A popular story from Disneyland's earliest days tells of a trip Walt once took on the Jungle Cruise, Adventureland's original and signature attraction. Each excursion was supposed to take seven minutes, but boat captains frequently went faster, especially on hot summer days with hundreds of people queued up waiting on the dock. Walt himself was a passenger on one of these abbreviated adventures and came looking for Dick Nunis, the lead cast member responsible for the ride. In his book *Window on Main Street*, Van Arsdale France, who was responsible for all original cast member training, recounts what happened next:

> "Dick, what is the trip time for this attraction?" "Well, sir, it is seven minutes,"' Dick responded. Mad as hell, Walt came back with, "Well, I just had a four-minute ride and went through the hippo pool so fast I couldn't tell if they were rhinos or hippos." After being completely chewed out by Walt, Dick made a very bright career decision. He asked Walt if he had time to ride with him and explain how he wanted the ride to work. Walt took the time.... A week later, Walt came back for a review. Dick recalled, "Walt felt I might have stacked the deck with the best operator, so he went around with five different hosts.... When he finally left after his last trip, Walt gave me a smile and a 'thumbs up' sign. I'd learned a valuable lesson."

YOU CAN ONLY IMAGINE

I AM FORTUNATE. I LEARNED the importance of emotional, E-ticket experiences early in my tenure as an educational leader. Within my first month as campus dean in Southeast Arizona, we were scheduled for a graduation. I bristled at the prospect of being responsible for such a ceremony. I was always bored at my own graduations, but now I found myself responsible for presiding over the pretentious protocol that I loathed. There was no way this was going to end well.

Knowing it would be impossible for me to get graduation right on my inaugural run, I decided to focus my energy and efforts on the reception that followed. The university was Baptist, of the Southern variety, so having phenomenal food would no doubt cover for the multitude of sins I was sure to commit during Commencement.

We ordered EVERYTHING: nuts and mints, veggie trays, cookie trays, and enough sheet cakes with the words "Congratulations Graduates" to feed an invading army. And we made sure we had on hand a plethora of punch (punchless, of course).

The graduation went off without a hitch. It wasn't great by anyone's standards, let alone my own, but it allowed me to keep my job and focus on getting better for the next ceremony in a short six months.

The reception, however, was flawless. People were happy and mingling with more than enough food to keep them distracted and satisfied. Eventually, everyone began filing out of the auditorium and it was time to commence with cleaning. It was then that I realized we had exceeded our own expectations. We had enough food left over to supply a small soup kitchen for well over a week. As I was standing there, perplexed with this problem, a woman came up to me and asked, "What are you going to do with all of that food?" Great question!

"We don't have a plan," I replied. "We never anticipated having so many leftovers."

"Mind if I take them?" she asked.

"No, of course not," I said. "Anything is better than throwing away all of this food."

I offered to help her carry everything out from the auditorium and to her car. After multiple trips, I asked her, "What do you plan on doing with all this food?" My first thought was that she did, in fact, work at a homeless shelter or a soup kitchen. Perhaps, given that it was a Saturday afternoon, maybe she had an event on Sunday and was trying to save money for her congregation by procuring free food. She set another tray of cookies down in her car, turned around, and smiling from ear-to-ear, proclaimed that she was throwing a graduation party for her brother! "Oh great," I responded. "That's exciting!"

Allowing my curiosity to get the best of me, I then asked one question further. "Well, congratulations on your brother graduating today. That is awesome! But tell me, what were you and your family going to do for food at this party if we hadn't had all of these leftovers?"

She responded with words I will never forget. "Oh, Dr. Barnes, we hadn't planned that far ahead. This is my brother we are talking about. No one *ever* imagined that he would *ever* actually graduate!"

And so began the first of many emotional, E-ticket experiences in my educational career. For the next graduation, we began collecting pictures of our graduates: kindergarten, high school, wedding, family, career, deployments, you name it. All of these were then turned into a video set to the then popular Mercy Me song, "I Can Only Imagine." Every graduation ended on this note. I would set it up with the "No one *ever* imagined that he would *ever* actually graduate" story. We would then cue the song and families would wait in anticipation as their respective graduates' stories played out on screen. Applause erupted with each image, and by the time the song was finished, there wasn't a dry eye in the place.

I want to encourage you to challenge yourself, challenge your organization, and challenge your corporate culture to strive constantly for emotional, E-ticket, exceptional "WOW" experiences. If it helps, you can even think of WOW as the "Wisdom of Walt." What would your life, your company, your sales, your success look like if you constantly created these kinds of W.O.W. E-ticket experiences?

You can only imagine!

SOUVENIR STOP

THE E-TICKET IS NOW EXTINCT. Disneyland eliminated the ticket book system in 1982 and admission now covers the price of all rides, show, and attractions. But good customer service should never become extinct. Let's take what we have learned from Walt in this chapter and use it to set ourselves, and our businesses, apart from all the others.

PLAN ON "PLUSSING"—IMPROVING THE GUEST experience became synonymous with Walt Disney and Disneyland. For most of us, the word "plus" is a noun. Walt, however, turned it into a verb. "Plussing" was Walt's way of always looking to make Disneyland and his guests' experience more pleasurable.

Walt walked the park most frequently on Saturdays, the busiest day of the week. He wanted to see what his guests were seeing, hear what his guests were hearing, and experience what his guests were experiencing. Regardless of your business or company, job or position, make a commitment over this next week and plan for a "plussing" day. Be your own guest, consumer, and customer, and find at least three ways to enhance their experiences. Write down your "plussing ideas below:

1. ____

____

2. ____

____

3. ____

____

"Whenever I go on a ride,
I'm always thinking of what's wrong with the
thing and how it can be improved."

— Walt Disney

Look for Loyalty—Disney and Disneyland must be doing something right. At current count, over 650 million guests have experienced Disneyland. At Disney World, 70 percent of guests are repeat visitors. Answer the questions below to see whether you and your company are simply providing a satisfactory experience or one that leads to loyalty and the promise of return visits.

1. How can you better help your employees understand that your customers are *their* paycheck?

___

___

___

2. Who is your *happiest* employee? How can you use him or her as an example for others? Attitude is everything. Sometimes, it really is that simple. Hire people who are happy!

___

___

___

3. How can you focus on the *experience* as much as you do the product? Remember, when it comes to product versus experience, people are willing to pay a premium for an exceptional experience.

___

___

___

4. Reflect on how you *treat* your team. Do you treat your team the way you expect your team to treat your customers? In my career, we like to say, "The campus takes on the personality of the dean." Make sure your persona is what you want your team members portraying to your customers.

____

____

____

5. How can you help your team stand on *principles* rather than hide behind policies? Your customers *might* be interested in what you stand for and what you believe in. They couldn't care less, however, about your policies. Your team members are there to solve problems, not to train customers on policies.

____

____

____

TAKE INVENTORY—DO YOURSELF A FAVOR and take a quick inventory using the "coupon books" below. On one book, I want you to list your top five "A, B, C, D, & E" possessions. Now on the second book, I want you to list your top five "A, B, C, D, & E" life experiences. Which book means the most to you? Which is filled with more memories? Which ticket book holds the most value?

POSSESSIONS
A. ______________________________
B. ______________________________
C. ______________________________
D. ______________________________
E. ______________________________

LIFE EXPERIENCES

A.____
B.____
C.____
D.____
E.____

GETTING YOUR HAND STAMPED

PART OF THE RUSH TO open Disneyland on July 17, only one year after the groundbreaking, was to ensure a flow of cash during the critical, summer tourist season. With all of the construction challenges, some argued for a delayed September opening, but Walt could ill afford to wait. He had poured every penny, and more, into his Disneyland dream. If he missed the receipts from that first summer season, Disneyland might not be around for a second.

Because of Walt's investment in the guest experience, today the park has almost zero "off-season." In fact, the busiest two weeks aren't even during summer anymore but rather take place in winter, during Christmas break. The park is so popular during this peak period that it is not at all uncommon for Disneyland, in the interest of guest experience, to close its gates and, unfortunately, turn prospective patrons away as early as 11 a.m.

The tradition of "plussing" the park for the holidays started, of course, with Walt. According to Bob Thomas in *Walt Disney: An American Original,* in 1959, the first Christmas season after the aforementioned six-million-dollar expansion of Tomorrowland, and with attendance having already exceeded anyone's wildest expectations, Walt wanted to spend another $350,000 on a Christmas parade. His managers argued against it. Hadn't they spent enough already? Besides, unlike an actual attraction with its requisite tickets, a parade wouldn't even generate revenue. Walt rejected their arguments and countered their complacency, "We can't be satisfied, even though we'll get the crowds at Christmastime. We've always got to give 'em a little more. It'll be worth the investment. If they ever stop coming, it'll cost ten times that much to get 'em back."

The lesson? Give the gift of experience to yourself, your spouse, your children, your team, and your customers. Give the gift of experience All Year Long.

STARTING EARLY

"The way to get started is to quit talking and begin doing."

MY DISNEYLAND SCAR

DISNEYLAND HELPS GUESTS CELEBRATE A variety of special occasions with free buttons. It is not at all uncommon to see guests wearing proclamations such as "I'm Celebrating," "Just Married," "Happy Anniversary," "Graduate," or even "First Visit." This practice is relatively new and certainly wasn't around when I first entered the park over twenty-five years ago. Instead of having a "First Visit" button tucked away as a sacred heirloom, I simply wear the scar from my first visit. It is a constant reminder of one of life's most important lessons, one that is critical to enjoying a day at Disneyland: Start Early.

On my first visit, I hated Disneyland. The visit was a disaster. Okay, nobody died and we *were* at Disneyland, so my use of the word "disaster" is a bit of hyperbole. I have certainly experienced worse days. However, happiness is often measured by expectations, and my expectations for a vacation day in the Happiest Place on Earth were catastrophically high. Nonetheless, that initial experience taught me one of the most important lessons about both Disneyland and life.

Our family awoke on a Saturday morning in August and methodically made our way through showers, getting dressed, and preparing for our day. We stopped in at the hotel's restaurant and enjoyed a full, leisurely breakfast. Naturally, all we talked about was our excitement. None of us had ever been to Disneyland before and we couldn't wait to find out for ourselves what all the fuss was about.

Around 10 a.m., we made our way to the park. After parking our vehicle and purchasing our tickets, we finally found ourselves on Main Street around 10:30 a.m. Main Street, while impressive, didn't particularly interest me because a new, exciting attraction had just opened a few months earlier in Tomorrowland. Television commercials throughout California had been touting the wonders of Star Tours for months, so I couldn't wait to ride it myself.

We made our way to Tomorrowland as quickly as possible. As we turned right off of Main Street, I began suspecting trouble. We asked a cast member the location of Star Tours; we were in the right place for the *ride* but in the wrong location for the *line*. He directed us back toward Main Street and the end of what I would soon learn was a very long line.

Three hours later, I finally rode my first Disneyland attraction. Now, don't get me wrong; Star Tours is good, but not *three hours good*. This is more a statement about my lack of patience than the original quality of Star Tours. Niki is fond of saying that she has never once seen me lose my patience. After all, you cannot lose what you *do not have*!

We exited Star Tours into a hot, Southern California afternoon. The park was filled to overflowing. People and lines were everywhere. I remember also riding Space Mountain and Big Thunder Mountain but not much else. The day concluded with shopping on Main Street. What we needed most the park didn't sell: open space. Other than that, there really isn't much I remember from that first, ill-fated trip all those many years ago. So much for first impressions.

The lessons learned on that fateful day have never been forgotten. I have since read a gluttony of guidebooks and possess an array of apps, all aimed at helping you beat the crowds and avoid standing in line. Friends often ask me for advice and tips. After years of study and hundreds of visits to the park, it all comes down to two words: Start

Early. Or, as Walt once said, "A person should set his goals as early as he can and devote all his energy and talent to getting there."

PUTTING THE "PRO" IN PROCRASTINATION

PROCRASTINATION, THE DELAY IN DOING what you know must be done, is kryptonite to your ability to be super successful. I say this from personal experience. I put the "pro" in procrastination. I am really, really good at it.

For example, when it comes to the History of Disneyland class, I haven't been 100 percent truthful with you. Yes, the idea came to me one afternoon while lecturing on the 1950s in one of my United States History courses. The idea quickly became a dream, and from there, it became a vision that simply had to be realized. I often found myself daydreaming about what the class would actually be. I had a syllabus. I knew the topics we would cover. I vetted out all of the assignments. I knew the guest speakers I would invite and the field trips we would take.

All of this, down to the very last detail, existed exclusively in my head. I knew it was great. I knew it was awesome. First, however, I had to face my fears. Most importantly, I had to get started.

The mind that dreamed up the perfect class was the same mind that could sabotage me just as quickly:

> *"You teach at a real university."*
>
> *"There is NO WAY they are ever going to let you teach a class on Disneyland."*
>
> *"You will be laughed off campus for pitching the idea of such a Mickey Mouse course."*
>
> *"The idea of teaching Disneyland is a pass to the front of the line—the unemployment line!"*

My system of self-sabotage spent the next several years talking to anyone who would listen to "my great idea." Everyone loved it, everyone except for the people who could actually assist me in getting the course approved and on the schedule. I kept my dream safe by making sure I never said a word about it to anyone who mattered. All of this ended one memorable day in May.

We had just finished graduation and were settling into the sleepy season that is summer on a university campus. My mind was adrift with all that I *could* do with so much extra time on my hands over the next four months. Starting the approval process for my History of Disneyland course was at the top of my list. Monday passed, however, and I left my office thinking about how it could wait until Tuesday. Again. Tuesday was the equivalent of waiting for the entire summer. Procrastination knows no season.

As I was leaving campus and accelerating onto the freeway, I suddenly heard a noise. I looked into my rearview mirror just in time to see my cellphone doing cartwheels down the shoulder of the freeway. Oh no!

I raced up to the next exit, crossed over, got back onto the freeway going in the opposite direction, crossed over again, and then slowly began to make my way along that same shoulder of asphalt. Before I ever found my phone, I saw something else that looked painfully familiar. You see, in the midst of all of my distracted thinking, I had not only left my phone on the roof of my car, but my iPad as well.

As I stood there on the shoulder with about a $1,000 in shattered electronics in my hand, I realized it wasn't just cars passing me by. It was all of my goals, all of my dreams, and all of my aspirations that were rushing past me as well.

It was in that moment that I made *the* decision. I stopped thinking and started doing. One year later, I celebrated the anniversary of running over my electronics by giving the very first lecture in my History of Disneyland class. How did this happen? Because of my commitment to stop thinking and start doing.

PERFECTION VS. PROCESS

IN OUR CHAPTER ON PASSION, we saw how Walt was always committed to building some sort of amusement park. Once he committed to Anaheim and made his decision to build Disneyland, it only took one year from groundbreaking (July 1954) to opening day (July 1955). You can think and talk about doing something forever. I suspect your dream, your goal, or your vision might not be quite as complicated as building the world's first theme park. Why not get started and let's see where you are 365 days from now?

I know, you want it to be perfect. Perfectionism is the root cause for procrastination, at least for me. What I have learned, and what I teach my students, is that before perfection (assuming perfection is even possible), you must first have process. Your process begins when you stop talking about your ideas, dreams, goals, and visions, and you actually start doing. Once you take that first step, which is always the most difficult, you must then trust that where you start isn't at all where you will finish. You and your project are going through a process. And the best way to get through a process is simply to stop talking and start doing (wise words from Walt).

When Niki and I first moved to Southern California, I was amazed by the locals who were constantly telling us what we "couldn't" do. For example, we were excited about having immediate access to the beach, the mountains, and yes, of course, Disneyland. We enjoyed sharing this excitement with others, but it was often quickly squashed. "Oh, you won't be going to Disneyland nearly as often as you think. The freeway is a parking lot day and night." "Don't even think about going to the beach. You will never find a parking spot." "The mountains? Forget it! The traffic is hell regardless of whether you are going up or down."

Amazingly enough, we have sat in very little traffic during our first few years in Southern California. Now don't get me wrong. Southern California is crowded, and the freeways, like everything else, are certainly congested. The key, of course, is starting early.

Starting early may well be the most memorable lesson from my History of Disneyland course. College students are like cats, notoriously nocturnal, and everything is on their terms. When they learned we were meeting at the park at 7:30 to make "rope drop" on Main Street by 8 a.m., I faced a near mutiny. None of them even knew what rope drop was because no one had ever arrived at the park early enough to experience it opening.

When we met around the planter near Gate 13, the lines to enter the park were relatively short, but the students believed it already looked "crowded." "No worries," I responded. "Disneyland is a big park so it will absorb everyone here for early entry quick enough." What followed was the "Best Disneyland Day" any of them had ever experienced. We went from attraction to attraction, well ahead of the massive crowd that began arriving in earnest some two hours after our head start. By 2 p.m., my students declared that they had accomplished more in half a day, by starting early, than they had ever accomplished on any other day at Disneyland. They promised me it was a lesson they would never forget. In fact, many of them assured me that the next time they visited the park, they would be sure to be there, with friends and family, at opening.

As a leader, I certainly wish I had known at twenty what I now know at fifty. It isn't about being smart. You may well be the smartest person in your family, your class, or even your company. It is about knowledge. And knowledge comes with repetitions.

One way we can speed this process up is by applying the lesson my students learned on our field trip to "Start Early." You may be thinking, "Great advice. I wish I had known this thirty years ago. What good does it do me now?" I believe that we all have the opportunity to start early with each and every new day. Be it exercise, meditation, a creative project, or the task you least look forward to facing, all of the experts implore us to get these things done first.

None of us can start our lives over. What you can do is commit to *starting early* each morning. Every day provides us with the opportunity to hit our own personal restart button. Each year represents a 365-page book that is unwritten and unedited.

SOUVENIR STOP

Start—Okay, I know this is confusing. This section is supposed to be our "Stop" and yet I am beginning with "Start." What gives?

One of the most influential books I have ever read is Jon Acuff's *Start: Punch Fear in the Face, Escape Average, and Do Work that Matters.* Like my favorite attraction at Disneyland, Space Mountain, I keep returning to this book again and again. Here is a highlight from it:

> The starting line is the only line you completely control. The start is the only moment you're the boss of. The finish? Don't kid yourself. That's months, if not years, away. You are going to meet dozens of people who are going to impact your finish. You are going to have countless opportunities, experiences, and challenges that dot the map of awesome you're following. There are cliffs and rivers and jungles you can't begin to fathom. You are going to stand on a mountaintop that is better than anything you ever dreamed and laugh at the idea that you thought you could plot out your finish. The start? You own that, son. That's yours."

What can you do today? Right now? This instant that represents your version of Start?

Now!

I don't mind waiting. I will be here waiting when you return. Just use the space below to write down your Start, but only *after* you have started.

___

___

___

___

Now, reflect on the following Acuff question: "What do you do when all the excuses you used to not chase your dream are gone? What do you do then?" In the space below, list your excuses.

____

____

____

____

Now I want you to write down the exact actions you would take if *none* of these excuses existed. These actions represent the follow-up to your start. Don't be sad. Be busy. Dreams are realized by action, not excuses.

____

____

____

____

Oddly enough, the day I ran over my electronics, I had started reading Acuff's book that morning.

Coincidence?

According to Albert Einstein, "Coincidence is God's way of staying anonymous." Speaking of anonymity....

Procrastinators Anonymous—Hi, my name is Jeff. I am a member of Procrastinators Anonymous (P.A.). Okay, this book is selling really well so maybe not so anonymous anymore. Nonetheless, please know that you are powerless to break your procrastination problem alone. Over time, procrastination isn't a choice anymore. It is a habit. Habits need help. You need support. Our office formed a Procrastinators Anonymous group. We meet weekly, and the book you are reading is a product of our efforts. We hold each other accountable for small tasks, e.g., calling the bank, going to the DMV, or returning a pair of shoes before the receipt expires. I know it sounds silly, but I suspect it also sounds familiar?

Soon enough, P.A. wasn't just about returning a pair of shoes on time. We learned that each of us wanted to walk in bigger and better shoes. Transparency brought trust, so we began sharing our real dreams, goals, and visions, and how our propensity for procrastination was perpetually holding us back. My P.A. buddies deserve enormous credit for keeping me accountable for writing this book. If you don't know where your "Start" should be, start by forming your own Procrastinators Anonymous. You have room to write the prospective names of your group members below.

____

____

____

____

"Everyone needs deadlines. Even the beavers. They loaf around all summer, but when they get faced with the winter deadline, they work like fury. If we didn't have deadlines, we'd stagnate."

— Walt Disney

Tomorrow(land) Is Not Your Friend—We procrastinators always see tomorrow as our BFF (Best Friend Forever). That isn't true, even at Disneyland. As stated earlier, during the park's construction, the Tomorrowland area was the last to be designed and the last to be constructed. It was woefully incomplete on opening day and has struggled, especially in comparison to the other lands, ever since. Too quickly, tomorrow becomes today and today becomes yesterday. It is impossible to keep up. As author and blogger Steven Guise says, "Tomorrow smiles and makes lofty promises to us, but when we wake up each morning, it vanishes and it's today again."

Today is the best predictor of what you will do tomorrow. That is why it is so important that you pick some sort of Start. Now. Today. Guise goes on to say, "We wrongly but persistently expect to make different decisions tomorrow than we do today." We all want our dreams and successes to be closer. Guess what? Today is *much* closer than tomorrow. So Start. Start Early.

"Most answers reveal themselves through doing, not thinking."

— Jen Sincero

GETTING YOUR HAND STAMPED

ONE OF THE MOST VALUED pieces of artwork in the Disney archives is the original sketch of Disneyland created by Herb Ryman. The sketch's history, often referred to as "The Lost Weekend" story, is the stuff of legend. Because this story was only told, and retold, after the fact, it exists in a variety of forms. I am going to share with you a paraphrased version, inspired by Werner Weiss' retelling at http://www.yesterland.com/ryman.html.

In September, 1953, Walt and Roy were ready to approach bankers about securing financing for Walt's dream of Disneyland. Walt had spent years talking about the park, but it still only existed in his head. They knew they needed to take something "concrete" with them to New York, so Walt called up former Disney Studio employee, Herb Ryman, one Saturday morning and invited him over. Once Herb arrived, Walt told him they were going to build an amusement park. Intrigued, Herb asked about the name. "Disneyland," Walt replied. Herb responded with, "Well, that's as good as any, I guess."

Walt told Herb that Roy was leaving for New York in less than two days. He would need a map, a drawing, something to show the bankers. "Those business men don't listen to talk, you know; you've got to show them what you're going to do." They then sprung it on Herb that they were hoping that he would do the drawing. Herb refused. "I can't do something like that on such short notice. It will embarrass me and ultimately embarrass you." Walt begged. "Herb, this is my *dream*. Please. What if I stayed here with you and we worked on it together?"

Once again, passion won out and Walt was successful in persuading Herb to stay. According to Michael Broggie in *Walt Disney's Railroad Story*:

> With each themed section, Walt carefully crafted—in precise detail—how it would work, mentally walking through every area and building, and riding on every attraction. His storytelling ability wove word pictures, from which Herb quick-sketched visual interpretations with a carbon pencil. For the next 42 hours, the two spent all of their imaginative and creative energy in a marathon session.

Here is the key point: Disneyland is recognizable in the original, bird's-eye view drawing. We can see such familiar sights as Main Street, The Hub, Fantasy Land, Frontier Country (Frontierland), and True-Life Adventureland. At the same time, there are also mystery locales such as Holiday Land, Recreation park, Lilliputian Land, and Mickey Mouse Club. What happened? Walt started, and over time, his process led him to something similar, but different, than his original concept. He didn't begin with perfection. He simply began with start.

"Errors accumulate in the sketch and compound in the model. But better an imperfect dome in Florence than cathedrals in the clouds."

— Leon Battista Alberti,
Fifteenth Century Architectural Theorist

WAITING IN LINE

"The difference in winning and losing is most often...not quitting."

YOUR EXPECTED WAIT TIME IS...

OBVIOUSLY, I BELIEVE DISNEYLAND TEACHES us a number of important life lessons. I find it necessary to relearn one of these lessons every day. Patience.

You have to be patient when visiting Disneyland. As we already know, you can start early and get ahead of the crowd, but if you stay for a full day, you are eventually going to have to learn to stand in line. Disneyland has mastered the art of the queue and trained its patrons to wait. In fact, for many of the more modern attractions, the queue may be as much a part of the show as the actual ride.

The Indiana Jones Adventure, opened in 1995, is a prime example. As mentioned earlier, the line begins in Adventureland, but as you traverse the queue, you actually go underneath the berm and into a show building that sits beyond the park's perimeter. All told, the queue for Indiana Jones is over an eighth of a mile long, and parts of it are as detailed as any other area in Disneyland. If you miss the line at Indiana Jones, then you have actually missed a major part of the attraction.

Despite the attempt to make standing in line as alluring as possible, people still complain about the crowds and inevitable long waits.

As a result, the past decade has seen a number of innovations to assist guests in maximizing their day at Disneyland. Every year, Bob Sehlinger, Seth Kubersky, and Len Testa publish a new edition of *The Unofficial Guide to Disneyland*. A major focus of their guide centers on crowd calendars and their recommendations on when to go. They even include touring plans and access to online resources that, in the 2013 edition, promise to "save you 4 entire hours of waiting in line." Because of my propensity for impatience, I have purchased multiple copies of their guides over the years and have found their advice to be invaluable.

In 1999, Disneyland introduced its *FASTPASS* system, a new approach to the dilemma of guests waiting in long lines. *FASTPASS* is a free ticketing system that affords guests the opportunity to wait for an attraction via a "virtual queue" while enjoying other aspects of the park. A *FASTPASS* gives you a scheduled time to return to the attraction, with a one-hour window of flexibility, that pretty much puts you at the front of the existing standby line. Knowing how to use the *FASTPASS* system can go a long way to keeping you on rides, out of line, and maximizing the magic. Know, however, that the system isn't perfect, it has its limits, and before the end of your day, you will still end up waiting in line(s).

YOU CAN'T *FASTPASS* SUCCESS

LIKE LIFE, NOT EVERY ATTRACTION has a *FASTPASS*. Success takes time, and dreams don't become true overnight. If you have not already experienced waiting, you will, so know going in that patience is required. Regardless of how early, or excited, you might start your day at Disneyland, the lines are inevitable. The same is true with life, leadership, and success. In his book *The War of Art*, Steven Pressfield encourages us to think of the internal obstacles that keep us from our goals as "resistance." Pressfield writes, "Resistance outwits the amateur with the oldest trick in the book: It uses his own enthusiasm against him. Resistance gets us to plunge into a project with an overambitious and unrealistic timetable for its completion. It knows we can't sustain that level of intensity. We will hit the wall. We will crash." In other words, you *will* wait in line.

The good news is that while you are waiting, you will be keeping good company. Walt Disney stood in line—a lot. At Disneyland, he was fond of disguising himself so he could enjoy his park like an everyday guest. This meant that he, too, stood in line. Walt's main reason for being an "average Joe" was so he could immerse himself in the guest experience. His disguises enabled him to gather objective data without skewing the results because cast members knew "The Boss" was riding. He also disguised himself to avoid the attention that comes with being a celebrity. By the time Disneyland opened, Sunday night broadcasts of *Disneyland* had made Walt a familiar figure in millions of Americans' living rooms so guests at Disneyland often went looking for The Man himself, Walt Disney.

In *How to Be Like Walt*, Williams and Denney recount the following memory of Art Linkletter:

> One time, Walt and I stopped by the Magic Shop on Main Street We bought fake beards and mustaches and put them on as a disguise. We strutted down Main Street, but the disguises didn't help. In fact, they probably just drew attention to us. We hadn't gotten very far when we were completely surrounded. So we gave out autographs and finally got away. Funny thing, though—not one of those people asked us, "Why are you wearing those beards?"

In truth, Walt Disney spent his entire life waiting in line. Success came neither easily nor instantly. When it did arrive, be it with Oswald the Rabbit, Mickey Mouse, or Snow White, either an external hurdle would materialize, e.g., Universal stealing Oswald, or more likely, Walt would want to risk the spoils of success to launch the company to the next level. This risk-taking created constant friction between him; his wife, Lilly; and his brother/partner, Roy. Especially Roy. According to the Disney Family Museum, it was only a few years before his death when Walt finally received the trust and validation he so richly deserved, as Walt related:

> After a long concentration on live-action and cartoon films, we decided to try something that would employ about every trick we had learned in the making of films. As the original *Mary Poppins* budget of five million dollars continued to grow, I never saw a sad face around the entire studio. And this made me nervous... no negative head-shaking. No prophets of doom. Even Roy was happy. He didn't even ask me to show the unfinished picture to a banker. The horrible thought struck me—suppose the staff had finally conceded that I knew what I was doing?

LIFE'S LONGEST LINE

I AM CURRENTLY STANDING IN what seems like the longest, most interminable line of my life. As I write this book, in an ironic twist that only switchback lovers can appreciate, I currently cannot ride anything at Disneyland, at least not any of my favorites. I am in queue until July 24, 2016 (not that anyone is counting).

In August 2014, ten days after my brain surgery, Niki and I returned to Los Angeles for a post-operative appointment. Returning to work was still weeks away, but I was already feeling better, so I asked when it would be okay for me to go back to Disneyland.

"Go back and do what?" my surgeon asked.

Realizing I had just broken one of my cardinal rules, i.e., "Never ask a question you don't already know the answer to," I murmured and stammered my reply.

"Well, um, you know, um, go back and ride, like, um, well, rides?"

"Two years!"

Feigning an appointment with an audiologist rather than a neurosurgeon, I exclaimed, "Excuse me?"

"Two years," he repeated. "Over the next twenty-four months, you must not ride anything that is going to shake you, spin you, jar you, drop you, or put any sort of significant G-force on you."

"Why?" I gasped.

"You *had* brain surgery. A craniotomy. We took a metal rod and bored it inches into your skull. It is going to take a full two years for your head to heal. If you get on one of those rides, you will die. It will kill you. We've done the research. Don't do it. Understand?"

Still not wanting to comprehend, I looked over at Niki. She was already in full-bore "Niki the Nazi" mode, so I knew it was over. Two years meant exactly that, two years. On the car ride home, we discussed the "no ride zone." It includes: Space Mountain, Star Tours: The Adventure Continues, The Indiana Jones Adventure, Pirates of the Caribbean (debatable in my opinion, but I lost), Splash Mountain, Big Thunder Mountain Railroad, The Matterhorn Bobsleds, Mad Tea Party (tea cups), Roger Rabbit's Cartoon Spin, California Screamin', Toy Story Midway Mania, Goofy's Sky School, Symphony Swings, Grizzly River Run, The Hollywood Tower of Terror, Luigi's Flying Tires, Mater's Junkyard Jamboree, and Radiator Springs Racers. The last one really gets me since I was actually riding in a car when it was determined that this Cars Land attraction is also off-limits.

But I will continue to wait because I know the payoff at the end of the line will be worth it. It always is.

SOUVENIR STOP

Remember Why You Are in Line—If you stand in line long enough, you can easily forget what it is you are waiting for. When the work gets hard and the days get long, it is easy to forget the payoff that waits for us upon completion. In the beginning, what was it that attracted you to your big goal or your big dream? Revisit that attraction from time to time and use it to encourage you as you keep pressing forward.

"Well, it took many years. I started with many ideas, threw them away, started all over again. And eventually it evolved into what you see today at Disneyland."

— Walt Disney

Enjoy the Queue—I have spent years wanting to be an author. Unfortunately, I had little interest in being a writer. People ask me all the time how I finally learned to write my book. My answer? By writing my book.

It may sound simple, but it really is the truth. The most important step you can take toward realizing your dream is showing up every day. Don't worry about how many days, months, or years it might eventually take. Today, you only have one job: show up.

When you do, I promise that you will enjoy the journey. Even before going to print, actually working on the dream of writing this book has already brought me the greatest sense of joy, happiness, success, and satisfaction I have ever known.

"Set for yourself any goal you want. Most of the pleasure will be had along the way, with every step that takes you closer."

— Jonathan Haidt, *The Happiness Hypothesis*

Manage Your Motivation—Attraction lines at Disneyland are all about capacity and loading procedures. High capacity attractions that continuously load, like "it's a small world", can carry up to 2,000 guests per hour. Lines for these kinds of rides can remain relatively short and are constantly moving, even on the busiest of days. Other attractions with low capacity and cyclical loading procedures (the full attraction must stop, off load, reload, and start again), like Dumbo the Flying Elephant, have constantly long and barely moving lines, even when crowds are light.

You will no doubt experience both: days when you accomplish more than you could ever imagine and others when it seems you barely moved at all. The key is to stay in line, regardless. Disneyland has "chicken exits" for those who cop out along the way. Success is not for the faint of heart.

"...at Disneyland, the queues were doubled back so that those in line would have a sense of advancing toward their goal and would see a constantly changing human vista."

— Bob Thomas, *Walt Disney: An American Original*

GETTING YOUR HAND STAMPED

By design, this is the shortest chapter in our journey together. In the interest of long lines and impatience, I want to move you along as quickly as possible. But first, I want to share with you a quick Disneyland tidbit.

On January 20, 1962, a rare cold and rainy Saturday in Southern California, Disneyland recorded its lowest attendance ever. Only 363 people walked through its gates. To put this in perspective, total attendance at Disneyland for 2012 was 16,202,000, an average of 44,389 guests per day. Imagine for a moment what it would be like to have "the place where dreams come true" almost all to yourself.

You can.

Everyone has dreams. We all want to be successful. The difference between dreaming and achieving is simply doing and never quitting. You have an advantage here because most people never start and even fewer finish. Stick to your goal and know that every step you take is distancing you ever further from the crowd.

"Every last one of us can do better than give up."

— Author Cheryl Strayed

BECOMING AN EDUTAINER

"I would rather entertain and hope that people learned something than educate people and hope they were entertained."

LEARNING YOUR ABC TELEVISION

As you know by now, Disneyland wasn't Walt's first Disneyland. Disneyland the place opened on July 17, 1955. But nine months earlier, Walt began the gestation period for the birth of the first theme park by premiering *Disneyland*, the television show. You wouldn't think people would need an education on how to have fun. Yet each week, Walt took people into the virtual classroom of *Disneyland* and schooled them on updates in Anaheim. Americans knew amusement parks, but Walt's ideas for Disneyland were so new, so different, and so radical that these concepts needed a weekly "show and tell" so the public could catch up with Walt.

When *Disneyland* premiered on ABC, it was largely because Walt and ABC needed each other; ABC was a fledgling network desperate for programming, and Walt, already turned down by the big boys at CBS and NBC, was desperate for financing to fund his dream. Like many others in Hollywood, Disney was initially skeptical of television and didn't want to weaken what was then his primary product, movies, by giving into the rigorous demands of creating programs on a weekly basis. However, he recognized, sooner than almost any of his peers, the tremendous potential of television and its ability to reach directly into the American home. According to Sam Gennawey in *The Disneyland Story,* "Most movie moguls felt the electronic box [television] would kill their businesses, and they shied away. Walt was not afraid. Just as he had done with sound, color, stereo, and so many other breakthroughs, he embraced technology."

In one of the first instances of product synergy, Walt's weekly show became an instant infomercial for the world's first theme park. Because nothing like Disneyland had ever been done, people were curious to see what Walt was up to in his new form of entertainment. By the time the park actually opened, Walt had done his job. His teaching style on Sunday evenings piqued interest and created a pent up demand for experiencing firsthand what so many viewers had watched unfold over the course of the previous months via television.

Despite needing a program to fund his dream and educate his audience, Walt believed that, "The idea of Disneyland is a simple one." Simultaneous with his television program, Walt also created a background piece that explained further the ideals of Disneyland, which became the foundation for Walt's dedication speech on opening day:

> The idea of Disneyland is a simple one. It will be a place for people to find happiness and knowledge.
>
> It will be a place for parents and children to share pleasant times in one another's company; a place for teacher and pupils to discover greater ways of understanding and education. Here the older generation can recapture the nostalgia of days gone by, and the younger generation can savor the challenge of the future. Here will be the wonders of Nature and Man for all to see and understand.

> Disneyland will be based upon and dedicated to the ideals, the dreams, and hard facts that have created America. And it will be uniquely equipped to dramatize these dreams and facts and send them forth as a source of courage and inspiration to all the world.
>
> Disneyland will be something of a fair, an exhibition, a playground, a community center, a museum of living facts, and a showplace of beauty and magic.
>
> It will be filled with the accomplishments, the joys, and hopes of the world we live in. And it will remind us and show us how to make these wonders part of our own lives.

ALWAYS A STUDENT

As an educator, I know many in academia who might find the idea of Walt Disney, a man whose formal education ended when he was only a freshman in high school, standing in front of a national audience and "teaching" a bit blasphemous. Where was his diploma? What were his credentials?

Walt had neither.

He never graduated from high school, nor did he ever attend college. In 1918, he quit school to join America's efforts in World War I and served in France where he drove ambulances for the Red Cross. His vehicles were unique because they weren't covered in camouflage; instead, Walt disguised them by covering them with cartoons.

Despite his lack of formal education, Walt Disney knew more about teaching and learning than I or many of my educated and credentialed colleagues in higher education. What were his secrets?

First, Walt understood the importance of lifelong learning and dedicated himself to this pursuit. As Williams and Denney state in *How to Be Like Walt*, "Like his heroes, Abe Lincoln, Thomas Edison and Charlie Chaplin, Walt was largely a self-educated man." Developing this discipline was a key to Walt's success and needs to be foundational to your own school for success. As the Disney Family Museum testifies, "Walt pieced together an education through his own life experiences, using the world as his classroom."

Secondly, Walt knew that having information is irrelevant unless you can find a way to make the information interesting and fun. If Walt Disney had a fear, it was the fear of boring his audience, and that fear drove his excellence as both an entertainer and educator. Disneyland is a unique classroom, a place where students have fun and find both education *and* happiness.

Lastly, Walt understood that he couldn't do everything. Sometimes, having an education isn't about what you know as much as it is about having awareness about what you *don't* know. Walt Disney knew his limitations, including his lack of formal education, and he never shied away from them. According to Bob Thomas in *Walt Disney: An American Original,* while Walt valued his many honorary degrees, including the three he received in 1938 following the success of *Snow White and the Seven Dwarfs* (a Master of Science from the University of Southern California and two Master of Arts degrees from Yale and Harvard University), he once remarked to his studio nurse, Hazel George, "I'd trade all my [honorary] degrees for your real one."

DEGREES OF DIFFICULTY

WALT'S "GAP" IN EDUCATION DID create its challenges, including problems with the proper pronunciation of words and names. His staff, too, was aware and tried to protect him from miscues by keeping known word challenges out of any camera scripts or meeting notes. For example, "drama" was "drammer" and the flying saucers in the old Tomorrowland attraction (where Space Mountain sits today) didn't "hover" they "hoovered." Walt may actually have been right about this one. The flying saucers never really worked, and thus, the attraction was relatively short-lived. Like a Hoover vacuum cleaner, the attraction "sucked."

Walt Disney holds the individual record for receiving the most Oscars—thirty-two—at the Academy Awards. On the Oscars' twenty-fifth anniversary in 1953, the Academy invited the acclaimed Walt to serve as an honorary presenter. That was the first year the awards appeared on television, and it did not go well for Walt. In *The Revised Vault of Walt*, Jim Korkis recounts:

> Walt mangled the names of several nominees. Miklos Rosza became "Miklos Rosca". Orchestra conductor Adolph Deutsch tried to loudly whisper to Walt the correct pronunciations from the orchestra pit, but it didn't help. Walt changed the song title "Am I in Love?" to "I Am in Love!", and couldn't make it all the way through Dimitri Tiomkin's name.

Before setting out to write this book, I thought I knew a lot about Walt Disney. I didn't know about his pronunciation struggles, however, and was very excited to learn these stories.

Why?

Because I, like Walt, have my own personal struggles with pronunciation. For example, I recently did a presentation on Disneyland, and when talking about the Davy Crockett Explorer Canoes attraction, I mistakenly pronounced them as the Davy *Crocker* Explorer Canoes. Part of me has always wanted to be like Walt, but sharing this non-fatal flaw may be as close as I can ever come.

I blame my mother, Evelyn, as the actual source of my malady. At her funeral (like Walt, she died at the relatively young age of sixty-five and within a few days of her birthday), all of the mourners enjoyed exchanging stories about their own favorite "Evelyn word." Examples include "extravaganza," which she pronounced "extravaganna," and "tentacle," which she pronounced as, yes, "testicle." No one ever had the balls to correct her, so we all just did our own internal translations and allowed her to move on with the conversation.

One Christmas, she visited my family in Southeast Arizona. We took a tourist day and headed over to the old copper mining town of Bisbee (oddly enough, the childhood home of Walt's studio nurse, Hazel George). After the mine closed in the 1970s, Bisbee transformed itself into a collection of New Age art, craft, and antique shops—Arizona's version of Santa Fe, New Mexico.

My mom always loved that sort of thing, so we were excited to take her. I figured she would need a full afternoon to explore the streets, mill around the shops, and take in the sights and sounds of this eclectic community nestled into the mountains just short of a mile above sea level. Much to my dismay, she declared herself finished in just under thirty minutes.

We then headed for the nearest restaurant and ordered lunch. While waiting for our meal, I asked Mom what she thought of Bisbee. I also commented on how hungry she must be, assuming, falsely, that was the answer for our aborted adventure.

She replied, "Hungry? This has nothing to do with hunger! I hate this place!"

Perplexed, I exacerbated the event by inquiring further. "Mom, there were arts, crafts, antiques—your kind of town. What could you possibly hate about Bisbee?"

Now aggravated, her animated audio response disturbed every other diner there that day. "There is incest here, Jeff! Incest! You can smell it in every store you walk in. If there is one thing I can't stand, you know it is the smell of incest!"

Remembering well the lessons of my youth, I didn't dare try to correct her. I knew from my childhood how "incensed" she became whenever anyone called her out on her improper pronunciations.

We have already discussed the significance of story in Walt's life and career. We also now know that story is at the center of why Disneyland exists. Story was central to Walt's ability to engage his audiences, and it is critical to your success as well. But beyond story is another aspect to Disneyland we must not forget. Walt didn't want to tell stories for the sole sake of telling stories. Walt pitched stories with purpose. Walt wanted stories that moved people, motivated people, inspired people, and, hopefully, educated them as well.

First and foremost, Walt recognized that learning doesn't start until fun begins. He never shied away from packing his parables with as much fun as possible.

THE HAPPIEST CLASSROOM ON EARTH

IN DISNEYLAND, WALT BUILT THE world's first, fully fun classroom. Folks who find out that I teach a college level course on the History of Disneyland either get it or don't. Those who get it want to take the class, wish they could take the class, or lament that no such class existed when they were in school. The other group consists of sad souls from the school of scoffers. As part of their inevitable inquisition, these people want to know whether we actually go to the park and spend a "class day riding roller coasters and eating churros." "Why yes, yes we do," I respond as I politely smile and move on to sharper and savvier souls.

I've come to realize that it is the fun that offends. Somehow, we've been tricked into believing that having fun is wrong, is reserved for kids, and that nothing we responsible adults do should entertain. If we find ourselves, God forbid, having fun, then it darn well better not happen during work or school.

Interestingly enough, I have developed over twenty different college level courses in my higher education career. The Fun Police don't want to hear this, but the History of Disneyland course is the *best* educational experience I have ever engaged in; the competition isn't even close.

The fundamental reason, I believe, is the inherent fun factor. We enjoy Disneyland. Our memories of it evoke emotion unlike any other shared public square. The idea that we can learn its story, experience life lessons, and hear about history, art, physics, and engineering means we have the opportunity for an unrivaled cross-disciplinary experience. That we have fun along the way means we are engaged from the start and form memories that last a lifetime, all without studying, memorization, or test taking. My student comments from End of Course Evaluations read as follows:

> "I loved and highly enjoyed taking this course! It was by far the best history class ever. I have never learned so much!" "This class was amazing!"
>
> "Excellent class! Far more academic than expected."
>
> "This class was great! I did not think I would learn all that I did. It was incredible the amounts of information that I ended up learning.... Absolutely loved it."
>
> "This was an AMAZING class.... Best class I have ever taken in the 4 years at CBU!"
>
> "I enjoyed this class more than any other I have taken at CBU. It was a true 400 level class, and I learned a lot about the history of our culture and society as well as important lessons I can apply to my life to help me succeed. I feel I learned information in this class that will follow me past CBU more so than any other.... I know it will benefit other college students just as it has benefited me.... This is also the only class where other students and I have requested the class sessions could be longer."
>
> "This has been by far the class I have learned and retained the most information in...."
>
> "Not only was this class extremely interesting, it was also informative. I do not feel like I have learned and retained as much information in other classes as I did in this class."

> "I have never wanted to go to class as badly as I wanted to come to this one. I was never not engaged in the topics we were learning.... [T]his class has been my favorite class I have ever taken...."

I have spent years in the classroom as both a student and as an educator. With certainty, I can say that Disneyland is the best classroom I have ever experienced. I have shared with you a few words from my students following our History of Disneyland class. We already know, however, that story speaks louder than data, so now allow me to share with you a story from one of our class field trips.

Excited by their experiences in class, my students asked whether it was okay to invite friends and family members to join us on our daylong tour of Disneyland. Tapping into my long-lost dream of being a Disneyland tour guide, I readily agreed. Our class doubled in size that day, and our guests, all Annual Passholders, shared an equally keen interest in the facts, history, and details of Disneyland that I pointed out on our route. Parents, many of whom were paying the tuition bills for their respective son or daughter, heartily thanked me for allowing them to share in the experience and for creating such a unique educational opportunity.

Toward the end of our tour, a father pulled me aside on the sidewalk of Main Street. "Before we go, I want to thank you for everything. My daughter loves your class. We have been going through some tough times of late. Without question, today is the *best day* we have ever shared together. Again, thank you."

Without question, to date it was my best day as an edutainer. According to Shane Snow in his book *Smartcuts*, Finland, a Scandinavian country with a population equivalent to the number of people living in Minnesota (*brr* for both) is excelling in the arena of education, especially math, science, and reading. The Finns have gained their top ranking by employing less effort, fewer classes, fewer tests, and less homework. But guess what they do have more of...and no, it isn't money. The Finns simply have more fun. They have discovered what Walt tried to teach us many, many years ago.

"Laughter is no enemy to learning."

— Walt Disney

SOUVENIR STOP

AT THIS POINT, YOU MIGHT be asking yourself whether being an edutainer is about teaching or learning.

Yes.

Let's use our Stop to challenge ourselves to do both. In this section, each suggestion is summarized with wise words from Walt.

GO BACK TO SCHOOL—REGARDLESS OF how many degrees you do, or do not have, never stop learning. Walt used the world as his classroom so school was always in session. Take a moment and write below something you have always wanted to learn or a place you have always wanted to go. Give yourself a deadline and make sure you don't skip class!

____

____

____

____

Me? I earned a band letter in high school for my years of playing saxophone. Truthfully, I've always wanted to play the drums. Maybe it is time for me to take some lessons. Who knows, after being dubbed "Dr. Disneyland," maybe someone will one day drub me "Dr. Drummer?"

"If you keep busy, your work might lead you
into paths you might not expect. I've always operated like

the princes of Serendip, who went on quests not knowing what they would find."

— Walt Disney

Be A Master Mentor—As you continue down your path toward success and enhance your leadership skills, you will develop lessons and experiences that others will need to know and only you can share. Who in your office, your family, or your circle of friends could benefit from your time and wisdom? Write down their names and give yourself one week to reach out and connect.

____

____

____

____

____

____

Just a few years before his death, and despite his supposed lack of education, Walt Disney started his own school. In 1961, he founded The California Institute of the Arts, or CalArts, as "the first degree-granting institution of higher learning in the United States created specifically for students of both the visual and the performing arts." It is located in Valencia, about as many miles north of Los Angeles as Anaheim is south. Alumni and attendees include such luminaries as: Dustin Hoffman, Tim Burton, and John Lasseter.

"It's the principal thing I hope to leave when I move on to greener pastures. If I can help provide a place to develop the talent of the future, I think I will have accomplished something."

— Walt Disney

BROWSE YOUR BOOKCASE—YOUR LIBRARY TELLS your story. During his lifetime, Walt Disney built his library both at home and at work. You need to follow Walt's example. According to Kathy Merlock Jackson, in *Walt Disney, from Reader to Storyteller,* "Disney prided himself on being a self-made man and used books when he needed them, in a goal-oriented, self-directed way to obtain information, figure out how things worked, and achieve a purpose."

First, thank you for reading this book! But what else have you read? What else do you need to read? Make two lists of five. First, list the five most important books you have ever read. Why? What were the lessons? Is it time to re-read them and re-experience those journeys?

1. ______________________________

____

2. ______________________________

____

3. ______________________________

____

4. ______________________________

____

5. ______________________________

____

Now, make a second list. This time, name five books that you know you need to read. Commit to reading them over the next six months. If you need a place to start, check the back of our souvenir shop (this book) for a list of recommended resources.

1. ______________________________

____

2. ______________________________

____

3. ______________________________

____

4. ______________________________

____

5. ______________________________

____

"There is more treasure in books than in all the pirates' loot on Treasure Island and at the bottom of the Spanish Main... and best of all, you can enjoy these riches every day of your life."

— Walt Disney

GETTING YOUR HAND STAMPED

WALT DISNEY WAS BOTH A student of history and a perpetual purveyor of progress. Main Street, USA reflects well his beloved boyhood home of Marceline, Missouri, and Walt's struggle with the nostalgia of the past and the hope of a better tomorrow. According to www.JustDisney.com, "Walt was our bridge from the past to the future." Personally, I can't help but wonder how many times Walt wandered down Main Street and made his own mental journey back home to Marceline.

According to Jim Korkis in *The Vault of Walt: Volume 2,* a year after Disneyland opened, in 1956, Walt and Lilly, along with Roy and his wife Edna, returned for real to Marceline. The city of 3,172 celebrated July 4 by honoring their hometown hero and dedicating the Walt Disney Municipal Park and Swimming Pool. While there, Walt visited the two-story, red-bricked school where his formal education first began. With photographers gathered around, he squeezed into his old, first-grade desk and proudly showed off his handiwork; he had carved his initials, "WD," into the desktop one afternoon while ignoring that day's lesson. He finally had something from a school he attended that showed he was there.

Walt Disney never earned a degree or diploma. Nonetheless, he left behind more than just his initials on an old school desk. His legacy includes that of educating and entertaining not only a country, but the world. What will your legacy be? What do you choose to leave behind?

Make your mark by being an edutainer.

HAVING A NEXT, ALWAYS...

"Disneyland will never be completed. It will continue to grow as long as there is imagination left in the world."

AS WE REACH OUR FINAL chapter and prepare to end our journey, I find it fitting that we find ourselves, like any day at Disneyland, right back where we started, on Main Street, U.S.A. Before we go, let's duck back into a familiar location, the Main Street Opera House. It was here that we began our journey and explored the famed bench from Griffith Park along with the attraction, Great Moments with Mr. Lincoln. If you explore just a bit further, you will also discover a giant map that models Disneyland on its opening day: July 17, 1955. I love any map of Disneyland, and this one is a personal favorite because you can easily see how much the park has grown and changed over these many years. Growth and change was a part of Walt's overall grand plan and vision.

Walt Disney liked to tinker with things. Ever the perfectionist, it perplexed Walt when one of his movies was done and it was time to seal the can and ship it for distribution to movie houses around the country. He was always thinking of ways to improve a story or edit an ending. Technology is always evolving. As a forward thinker, it was easy for Walt, in the 1950s, to imagine how current technology might enhance a film he had made back in the 1930s. But what was done was done, and once he sealed the can and shipped the film, it was time to move on to his next project. Walt moved on very quickly.

According to Jim Korkis in *The Revised Vault of Walt*, the morning after the successful premiere of *Snow White and the Seven Dwarfs*, animator Woolie Reitherman recalled: "I ran into Walt the next morning after the premiere. Instead of talking about how he could now take a little rest, he began talking about the next animated feature, and how he wanted to get started right away."

In Disneyland, Walt built the ultimate tinker toy, his own personal playground. It is a living, breathing, organic, story-making machine that is always advancing, evolving, and adapting. Think of the park as Walt's way of living on the set of his own live action movie, except he never had to worry about the director yelling, "Cut!" Disneyland is a story with no "can" and no "lid." Credit Walt Disney for finding a way to keep the film rolling.

Over the past sixty years, the world has enjoyed the evolution of Walt's dream. Today, Disneyland has well over sixty attractions, triple the number it opened with in 1955. Entire new areas have been added: New Orleans Square in 1966, Bear/ Critter Country in 1971, and Mickey's Toontown in 1993. A second park, Disney's California Adventure, opened in 2001 and ushered in the era of the Disneyland Resort. With all of this change, one cannot help but wonder whether Walt would even recognize his original dream today. The answer is yes.

Despite the park's evolution, original attractions still exist and remain central to Disneyland's DNA. When the park commemorated its Golden Anniversary in 2005, cast members honored these originals by painting portions of them gold and placing a "Class of 55" medallion on each. This list includes: Disneyland Railroad, Jungle Cruise, *Mark Twain* Riverboat, Casey Jr. Circus Train, Dumbo the Flying Elephant, The Storybook Land Canal Boats, King Arthur Carrousel, Mr. Toad's Wild Ride, Mad Tea Party (tea cups), Peter Pan's Flight, Snow White's Scary Adventure, Autopia, Main Street Cinema, and the Horse-Drawn Street Cars. Notice that the majority of these attractions are in Fantasyland, the heart of the park; today, Walt could walk through his beloved Disneyland without missing a beat.

Disneyland can change because its creator was always changing. Advancement was one of Walt's core values. He knew it was necessary always to have a next. According to film critic Leonard Maltin in the documentary *Walt Disney Treasures: Disneyland USA*, "Walt was never satisfied with the status quo. In his movie making or in his thinking about Disneyland." This concept was foundational to his success and is reflected in his lifelong list of achievements. Like Walt and like Disneyland, you also need your next. Regardless of where you find yourself today, you must never stop and never settle. Keep advancing. Keep evolving. Keep adapting.

Everyone needs a next.

DON'T GET HUNG OUT TO DRY

FOR MANY YOUNG PEOPLE, GOING to college represents the ultimate "next." This was certainly true for my daughter when she headed off to school, living on her own for the first time, at the age of seventeen. She adapted well. One incident early on, however, left me scratching my head and wondering whether she was truly ready.

After the first week on her own, she realized no one was there to do laundry for her. She headed off to the store to purchase what she would need to do it herself. Reaching for a bottle of liquid fabric softener, she decided to tinker with things, get outside her box, and become her own person. She grew up in a home that used liquid Downey exclusively. She had always wondered, however, about those things called "dryer sheets," especially the cute ones branded with the "Snuggles Bear." "*This is my chance,*" she thought. "*I am on my own. From this day forward, I am going to be a dryer sheet girl.*"

She finished her shopping and drove to the local laundromat. When the washers finished their final spin, she opened one up and discovered disaster: shredded dryer sheets scattered throughout clothes. She called me up, crying, convinced that her wardrobe was ruined. I tried to put a different spin on things by focusing more on her than the clothing. "Why would you put dryer sheets anywhere but in the dryer?" I asked. "Because I've only ever seen fabric softener go in the washing machine!" she replied.

Bethany learned. Eventually, she learned enough to graduate with a Bachelor's Degree in Creative Writing and a Master's Degree in Journalism. Her initial experience in evolution and adaptation may have been difficult (and funny), but she made it through her "next." You can, too. Don't stop. Don't settle. Otherwise, you risk waking up to learn that life has hung you out to dry.

LIVE LIFE ON THE FRONTIER

WALT DIED IN THE MIDST of his biggest dream ever. We know it today as Walt Disney World, but it was initially dubbed, "The Florida Project." Walt was never a fan of sequels, so he didn't really want to build a second Disneyland. In 1966, while giving his reception speech for the Showman of the Year Award, Walt shared the following: "By nature, I'm an experimenter. To this day, I don't believe in sequels. I can't follow popular cycles. I have to move on to new things. So with the success of Mickey I was determined to diversify. We kept fooling around with the *Silly Symphonies* until we came up with the *Three Little Pigs*. I could not possibly see how we could top pigs with pigs." So what was Walt really up to in Florida?

After revolutionizing the amusement park business with theming and adhering to the strictest standards of quality, service, and cleanliness, Walt now set his sights on urban planning. EPCOT, Walt's "Experimental Prototype Community of Tomorrow," was the true driving force behind Walt's vision for central Florida. Walt had already transformed how people *play*; now he wanted to revolutionize how we *live*. EPCOT did not open until 1982, sixteen years after Walt's passing. The final product looks far more like a traditional theme park/World's

Fair than the Experimental Prototype Community of Tomorrow Walt had envisioned. Nonetheless, EPCOT's existence is a testimony to the power of Walt's original vision and his commitment to never settling for the status quo and always having a next.

As much as Walt wanted to build the "Community of Tomorrow," the real lesson of EPCOT is the cutting-edge concept of always having a frontier. Granted, the idea of frontier, especially in the context of Disneyland, conjures up images and ideas from yesterday and years long ago. This concept is even echoed in Walt's own words when he dedicated Frontierland:

> It is here that we experience the story of our country's past. The color, romance and drama of frontier America as it developed from wilderness trails to roads, riverboats, railroads and civilization. A tribute to the faith, courage and ingenuity of our hearty pioneers who blazed the trails and made this progress possible.

But what if we challenge the limits of our thinking? Perhaps a frontier can be far more than a place? What if we move the boundary and make frontier a mindset? I am challenging you to picture yourself as a pioneer. Pioneers make progress. Don't just live off your stories of yesterday and accolades from years long ago. Instead, dedicate yourself to a life that is always moving forward. Pioneers do things they have never done and go places they have never been. Successful people know what Walt Disney knew—Frontierland is your friend.

This concept is not new. As an American History teacher, I lecture on the significance of frontier as foundational to the American story, a concept introduced by Frederick Turner at the Chicago World's Fair in 1893. (Yes, the same World's Fair where Walt's father, Elias, once worked.) Turner teaches us that having a frontier—uncharted territory and limitless land— frees us to think differently. This is the mentality President John F. Kennedy tapped into when he challenged America in the 1960s to go to the moon and tackle the final frontier: Space.

THE MELANCHOLY OF ALL THINGS DONE

I GREW UP DURING THE Space Age, and the adventures of our American astronauts enthralled me. I was only six at the time, but I vividly remember watching the Apollo 11 astronauts step onto the lunar surface for the first time on July 20, 1969. "That's one small step for man, one giant leap for mankind."

Then what?

If you need convincing that it is important always to have a next, then it is imperative that you know what followed. It isn't pretty. The first man on the moon, Neil Armstrong, spent the rest of his life trying to figure out what was next. According to Shane Snow in *Smartcuts*:

> Neil Armstrong...spent his next few decades figuring out what to do with his life. He briefly taught some small classes at a university, then quit unexpectedly. He consulted a little for NASA and some random companies, and did a commercial for Chrysler, and quit all those things, too. He hid from autograph seekers and sued companies for using his name in ads.

It was even worse for Buzz Aldrin, the second man on the moon. Once the buzz of walking on the moon wore off, Aldrin's life spiraled downward into depression and alcoholism. Buzz burned through three marriages and wrote multiple memoirs about his misery. In a January 2015 *Gentleman's Quarterly* article, "The Dark Side of the Moon," Aldrin is quoted as describing the mental breakdown that followed his return from the moon as "the melancholy of all things done." After all, what do you do after walking on the moon? Aldrin eventually answered this question with the following realization: "It's something we did. Now we should do something else."

Fortunately, Walt Disney never suffered from "the melancholy of all things done." He knew the importance of momentum and the necessity of frontiers and moving forward. On Disneyland's tenth anniversary in

1965, the same year he announced his "Florida Project," Walt shared with his team the following wisdom, "I just want to leave you with this thought, that it's just been sort of a dress rehearsal and we're just getting started. So if any of you start resting on your laurels, I mean just forget it, because...we are just getting started."

SOUVENIR STOP

WE HAVE REACHED OUR FINAL stop for souvenirs. Your bags are probably heavy, and you are no doubt nearly out of money. No worries. I will start by doing most of the work for you and my services are free of charge. I will then challenge you with a few questions to consider before you go.

In a *Los Angeles Times* article in January 2015, Brady MacDonald wrote about Disneyland's upcoming 60th birthday. He prophesied how the park might look on its centennial celebration in 2055. It is a curious piece of speculation. Playing the part of "armchair imagineer," MacDonald breaks the park down via its various lands and writes about which attractions in each area are "untouchable" versus those that are "vulnerable." Untouchables include such beloved classics as: Disneyland Railroad, Dumbo's Flying Elephants, Mad Tea Party (tea cups), King Arthur Carousel, "it's a small world", Matterhorn Bobsleds, Star Tours, Big Thunder Mountain Railroad, *Mark Twain* Riverboat, Sailing Ship *Columbia*, Jungle Cruise, Pirates of the Caribbean, and Haunted Mansion.

The list of vulnerable attractions is significantly longer, i.e., pretty much anything not listed above. The criteria for what should stay and what should go is highly personal and, again, significantly speculative. But that isn't the point. The idea that we can even play such a game and engage in such a debate is a reflection of the reality that Walt's dream really did come true. Disneyland really will never be finished. Even after Walt's death, only eleven years after the park's first opening, imagination has remained at Disneyland's core. The park has been advancing, evolving, and adapting ever since, and no doubt, it will continue to do so well past its Centennial Celebration.

I want you to stop and play the same game with your life. Be your own "armchair imagineer" and ask yourself these questions:

1. **Where will you be in one year?**

____

____

2. **Five years?**

____

____

3. **Ten years?**

____

____

4. **Take a look at your map and find Frontierland.** Where you have been can tell you a lot about where you are going. Do you like what you see? Why or why not? What course corrections must you make?

____

____

5. **Lastly, what are you doing now that is "untouchable" and will no doubt remain an attractive part of your ongoing story?** In turn, which areas are vulnerable and need to give way to new growth, new ideas, and new initiatives?

____

____

Sir Isaac Newton, the man who discovered gravity and first compiled the laws of motion, which ultimately made going to the moon possible, gave us a first law of success: "Objects at rest tend to stay at rest. Objects in motion tend to stay in motion." Success doesn't mean you are always doing something bigger or better. You just have to keep moving *forward*.

GETTING YOUR HAND STAMPED

PEOPLE OFTEN ASK ME WHAT my favorite Disneyland attraction is. The answer is Space Mountain. I have certainly been on more impressive roller coasters. And other Disney attractions have better theming and better detail. But for sheer fun, my far and away favorite is Space Mountain. During my current hiatus, it is certainly the attraction I miss the most. I have no doubt what I will be riding first when my restrictions are lifted on July 24, 2016—Space Mountain.

Walt's original plans for Space Mountain date back to 1964, but technology for the attraction lagged behind his imagination, so the mountain would have to wait for computers to catch up in the 1970s. The first Space Mountain was constructed at Walt Disney World's Magic Kingdom and opened in January 1975. Disneyland's would soon follow, opening on May 27, 1977, resulting in a Memorial Day Weekend record of 185,000 guests. Present for the launch of Disneyland's Space Mountain were six of the seven Mercury astronauts. (The lone exception was Gus Grissom, who perished in a launch pad fire in 1967.)

In advance of Disneyland's 50th anniversary celebration in July 2005, Space Mountain underwent an extensive and much-needed renovation. For two years, fans went without their "Space Mountain fix" while the entire attraction was gutted and rebuilt from the ground up. When it was time to re-launch the popular ride, and celebrate Disneyland's 50th birthday, Neil Armstrong was on hand and took the inaugural ride. Cast members presented him with a plaque that says: "Presented to Mr. Neil Armstrong for his courage and adventurous spirit that continues to inspire all mankind to reach for the stars." The plaque also features the Walt Disney quote "It's kinda fun to do the impossible."

You must launch and then launch again. What is your impossible next? Never rest on your laurels, and know that you are always only just getting started. Use your imagination and know, like Walt, "If you can dream it, you can do it."

CONCLUSION
NOW IT'S TIME TO SAY GOODBYE

FOR YEARS, DISNEYLAND COMMEMORATED CLOSING time by playing on its public address system "Now It's Time To Say Goodbye," the sign-off song from the 1950s television show, *The Mickey Mouse Club*. The song was Disneyland's way of thanking its guests for visiting, being company for the day, and encouraging you to return again.

Soon.

As you reach the end of this book, now is the time for me to say, "Goodbye." Like Disneyland, I, too, want to say thank you for being a part of this journey. I hope, however, that this is not a permanent goodbye. I want to encourage you to contact me and share what you liked, or disliked, about this book. Writing this book was a labor of love and a dream come true for me. I want to make it the best book possible so I need your feedback. Like Walt, I plan on "plussing" it for future printings and future readers. In your correspondence, don't hesitate to share with me your own Disneyland stories, but also other stories about you, your journey, and the obstacles, challenges, and adversities you are facing. My goal is to come alongside as many readers as possible and partner with you in living the best life possible.

My email address is Jeff@TheWisdomofWalt.com. I look forward to hearing from you, and responding back, soon.

Many guests don't realize it, but the shops on Main Street stay open a full hour after the park officially closes. Guess what this means? Even though I have already said my goodbye, you still have time for one more Souvenir Stop.

Yay!

SOUVENIR STOP

THROUGHOUT THIS BOOK, YOU HAVE learned some interesting facts and heard some memorable stories about Walt Disney and the magic of Disneyland's story. More importantly, I hope you have gained some of Walt's wisdom.

Now what? What do you do with that wisdom? It is time for you to take action!

Let me challenge you by asking you the following question: Imagine a family of five is riding the Disneyland Railroad and one family member decides to disembark at the next station. How many family members are left on the train?

Most people will answer "Four."

The right answer, however, is five. Before you scream that I can't do simple math, remember that *deciding* to do something is not the same as *actually* doing it. Again, you need to take action.

Let's practice some "package pickup" by taking a moment and reviewing the various "Souvenir Stops" from each chapter. From your review, use the lines below to highlight the ten actions you will commit to taking over the next ninety days as a result of reading *The Wisdom of Walt*. Walt Disney lived his dreams because he took steps—action—toward making those dreams come true. I don't know how many steps you are from your dream, but taking action—any action—will bring you one step closer.

1. ______________________________
2. ______________________________
3. ______________________________
4. ______________________________

5. ______________________________
6. ______________________________
7. ______________________________
8. ______________________________
9. ______________________________
10. ______________________________

BEFORE YOU GO

ONCE DISNEYLAND CLOSES, YOU NO longer need a handstamp. Nonetheless, I want to share with you one more story before you go and exit this book.

Late in Walt's career, people began to speculate that he might be interested in a political career. Why not? Given his success, popularity, and interest in problem solving, many presumed that politics would be a natural fit. When asked, Walt responded with one of my all-time favorite quotes, "Why be a governor or senator when you can be king of Disneyland?"

Walt wasn't born a prince. However, he lived his dreams, built his Magic Kingdom, and became king of Disneyland.

But what about you?

As the "Dean of Disneyland," I want to wish you the best in all that lies ahead for you. Like Disneyland, I want to challenge you to live a great story and to be your own hero. Dreams really do come true.

And not just at Disneyland.

—*Jeffrey A. Barnes*

ACKNOWLEDGMENTS

WALT DISNEY DID NOT BUILD Disneyland by himself. As Walt himself said, “To make the dreams of Disneyland come true took the combined skills and talents of hundreds of artisans, carpenters, engineers, scientists, and craftsmen.”

Just as Walt did not build Disneyland by himself, I did not write this book alone. I want to take a moment and acknowledge my team.

First, my wife, Niki. For years, she has put up with me talking about teaching a class on Disneyland and writing a book. Neither would have occurred without her inspiration, encouragement, patience, and willingness to weather my endless chatter about both. Thank you.

I also want to say thank you to our children, Bethany, Logan, and Wesley. Bethany, for your editorial ideas and for the risks you take in your writing every day. You started living your dream before me, and you have pushed me to the place I have always wanted to be: published. Logan and Wesley, for bearing with me when you ask what I am doing and my repeated response is “Writing.”

My dream of writing this book was just that, a dream, until I met my mentor and coach, Patrick Snow. Originally, coaches enabled people to get from where they were to where they wanted to be. Think Cinderella. Patrick, this is exactly what your coaching has done for me. Thank you!

I also want to express my appreciation to California Baptist University, especially Dr. Chris McHorney, Chair of our History and Government Department. Dr. McHorney was the first person to say, “Yes” to my idea of teaching a class on the History of Disneyland. It took years for me to build up the courage to ask. What I did not know, but have since learned, is that Dr. McHorney once worked at Disneyland as a cast member on the Davy Crockett Explorer Canoes, tipping the odds in my favor, no doubt. Thank you for your openness to my idea and your continued encouragement along the way.

I am also appreciative of Dr. Tracy Ward for her support, encouragement, and for granting me the time needed for getting the writing done. Thank you.

My team in Academic Services at California Baptist University deserves more than a few words of appreciation. Steve Neilsen, Mike Osadchuck, Pam Bailon, and Chelsea Sherwood, you are awesome people to work with. You supported this aspiration in every way possible and came alongside me to help make this dream possible. Thank you for playing such an instrumental part in the success that is this book. Hopefully, all of it "works." Congratulations to any of you who earned "Joke of the Day" for making fun of my writing and me. Paranoia can be so much fun! Who knew?

Speaking of paranoia, I also want to say thank you to Beverly. You understand well both me and the words of Anne Lamott, "I sat down to write and all of my mental illnesses showed up."

ABOUT THE AUTHOR

JEFF BARNES IS AN AUTHOR, professional keynote speaker, higher education administrator, university professor, and leadership/success coach. He has more than thirty-five years of professional speaking experience and nearly twenty years experience leading teams in higher education and teaching more than twenty different college courses in both the traditional classroom and online—including The History of Disneyland at California Baptist University in Riverside, California.

He attributes his passion for Disneyland to his love of history, story, and success. He believes the park teaches us some of life's greatest lessons—as long as you know its history, know what to look for, and you are willing to connect it all to your own story.

Jeff lives in Riverside with his lovely wife, Niki, and their two boys, Logan and Wesley. Their daughter, Bethany, lives in Las Vegas where she works as an investigative journalist at the *Las Vegas Review Journal*. When he is not teaching or writing, Jeff enjoys spending as much time as possible at "The Happiest Place on Earth."

VISIT JEFF ONLINE

- www.thewisdomofwalt.com
- jeff@thewisdomofwalt.com
- Jeff Barnes *or* The Wisdom of Walt
- @drdisneyland
- @drdisneyland

BOOK JEFF BARNES TO SPEAK AT YOUR NEXT EVENT

When it comes to choosing a professional speaker for your next event, you will find no one more energizing or fun—no one will leave your audience or colleagues with a more renewed passion and purpose for life—than Jeff Barnes. For more than thirty-five years, Jeff has been speaking, motivating, and inspiring nationwide.

Whether your audience is 10 or 10,000, Jeff Barnes can deliver a customized message of inspiration for your meeting or conference. Jeff understands your audience does not want to be "taught" anything, but is interested in experiencing stories of inspiration, achievement, and real-life people (such as Walt Disney) stepping into their dreams.

As a result, Jeff Barnes' speaking philosophy is to humor, entertain, and inspire your audience with passion, purpose, and stories to help people achieve extraordinary results. If you are looking for a memorable speaker who will leave your audience wanting more, book Jeff Barnes today!

To see a highlight video of Jeff Barnes and find out whether he is available for your next meeting, visit his site below. Then contact him by phone or email to schedule a complimentary pre-speech phone interview:

www.TheWisdomofWalt.com
Jeff@TheWisdomofWalt.com
520-227-9543

Jeff & Niki On their way to Club 33 inside Disneyland to celebrate their wedding anniversary, August 2013

TAKE A TOUR OF DISNEYLAND WITH DR. DISNEYLAND!

If you are going to Disneyland for the first time, or the 100th time, let Jeff Barnes be your guide. Jeff (and Niki) will be happy to meet you, your family, or your group on the day and time of your choosing. You will see the park in ways you've never seen it before and Jeff will enhance your magical experience by minimizing your wait times and maximizing your fun.

Contact Jeff today for pricing and availability:

Jeff@TheWisdomofWalt.com
(520) 227-9543

SEE YOU AT DISNEYLAND!

BIBLIOGRAPHY

BOOKS

Acuff, John. *Start: Punch Fear in the Face, Escape Average and Do Work that Matters*. Brentwood, TN: Lampo Press, 2013.

Broggie, Michael. *Walt Disney's Railroad Story*. Pasadena, CA: Pentrex, 1997.

Brokaw, Tom. *The Greatest Generation*. New York, NY: Dell Publishing, 1998.

Bryman, Alan. *Disney and His Worlds*. New York, NY: Routledge, 1995.

Canfield, Jack. *The Success Principles*. New York, NY: HarperCollins Publishers, 2005.

Capodagli, Bill and Lynn Jackson. *The Disney Way: Harnessing the Management Secrets of Disney in Your Company*. New York, NY: McGraw-Hill, 2007.

Cronkite, Walter. *A Reporter's Life*. New York, NY: Alfred A. Knopf, 1996.

Dietz, Karen and Lori L. Silverman. *Business Storytelling for Dummies*. Hoboken, NJ: John Wiley & Sons, Inc., 2014.

Finch, Christopher. *Walt Disney's America*. New York, NY: Abbeville Press, 1978.

France, Van Arsdale. *Window on Main Street: 35 Years of Creating Happiness at Disneyland Park*. Nashua, NH: Laughter Publications, Inc. 1991.

Gallo, Carmine. *Talk Like Ted: The 9 Public-Speaking Secrets of the World's Great Minds*. New York, NY: St. Martin's Press, 2014.

Gennawey, Sam. *The Disneyland Story: The Unofficial Guide to the Evolution of Walt Disney's Dream*. Birmingham, AL: Keen Communications, LLC, 2014.

Goins, Jeff. *The Art of Work*. Nashville, TN: Nelson Books, 2015.

Guise, Stephen. *Mini Habits: Small Habits, Bigger Results*. CreateSpace, 2013.

Haidt, Jonathan. *The Happiness Hypothesis*. New York, NY: Basic Books, 2006.

Jackson, Kathy Merlock and Mark I. West, Eds. *Walt Disney, from Reader to Storyteller: Essays on the Literary Inspirations*. Jefferson, NC: McFarland & Co., 2015.

Klein, Norman. *The Vatican to Vegas: A History of Special Effects*. New York, NY: The New Press, 2004.

Korkis, Jim. *The Vault of Walt: Volume 2*. Orlando, FL: Theme Park Press, 2013.

Korkis, Jim. *The Revised Vault of Walt: Unofficial, Unauthorized, Uncensored Disney Stories Never Told*. Orlando, FL: Theme Park Press, 2012.

Lefkin, Wendy, ed. *Disney Insider Yearbook: 2005 Year in Review*. New York, NY: Disney Editions, Inc., 2006.

Marling, Karal Ann. *Designing Disney's Theme Parks: The Architecture of Reassurance*. New York, NY: Flammarion, 1997.

Miller, Donald. *A Million Miles in a Thousand Years: What I Learned While Editing My Life*. Nashville, TN: Thomas Nelson Publishers, 2009.

Pressfield, Steven. *Do the Work!: Overcome Resistance and Get Out of Your Own Way*. The Domino Project, 2011.

Pressfield, Steven. *The War of Art: Break Through the Blocks and Win Your Inner Creative Battles*. New York, NY: Black Irish Entertainment LLC, 2002.

Sehlinger, Bob, Seth Kubersky, and Len Testa. *The Unofficial Guide to Disneyland 2013*. Birmingham, AL: Keen Communications, LLC, 2013.

Sincero, Jen. *You Are a Badass: How to Stop Doubting Your Greatness and Start Living Your Awesome Life*. Philadelphia, PA: Running Press, 2013.

Sklar, Marty. *Dream It! Do It!: My Half-Century Creating Disney's Magic*

Kingdoms. New York, NY: Disney Editions, 2013.

Smith, Dave, ed. *The Quotable Walt Disney*. New York, NY: Disney Editions, 2001.

Snow, Shane. *Smartcuts: How Hackers, Innovators, and Icons Accelerate Success*. New York, NY: HarperCollins Publishers, 2014.

Strayed, Cheryl. *Wild: From Lost to Found on the Pacific Coast*. New York, NY: Random House, 2013.

Tharp, Twyla. *The Creative Habit: Learn It and Use It for Life*. New York, NY: Simon & Schuster, 2003.

Thomas, Bob. *Walt Disney: An American Original*. New York, NY: Disney Editions, 1994.

Susanin, Timothy S. *Walt Before Mickey: Disney's Early Years, 1919-1928*. The University Press of Mississippi, 2011.

Weber, M. *Economy and Society*. 1925. 3 vols. G. Roth and C. Wittich, eds. New York, NY: Bedminster, 1968.

Williams, Pat and Jim Denney. *How to Be Like Walt: Capturing the Disney Magic Every Day of Your Life*. Health Communications Incorporated, 2004.

WEBSITES

https://bgavideo.wordpress.com/2008/10/23/disney-design-forced-perspective/

http://deepexistence.com/

https://disneyinstitute.com/blog/2013/10/letting-go-leadership-lessons-from-walt-disney/211/

http://findingmickey.squarespace.com/king-arthurs-carrousel-horses/

http://www.goodreads.com/quotes/556598-maybe-storiesare-just-data-with-a-soul

http://www.gq.com/entertainment/celebrities/201501/buzz-aldrin

http://www.hiddenmickeys.org

http://www.jonathanfields.com/life-is-a-contact-sport/

http://www.justdisney.com/walt_disney/biography/long_bio.html

http://www.laparks.org/dos/parks/griffithpk/mgr.htm

http://www.latimes.com/travel/themeparks/la-trb-disneyland-2055-20141223-story.html#page=1

http://www.leavingconformitycoaching.com/2013/06/berm-define-your-worldview.html

http://www.micechat.com

http://www.mouseplanet.com/8655/Tom_Nabbe_Is_Tom_Sawyer

http://www.ted.com/speakers/tim_brown

http://www.themedattraction.com/fastpass.htm

http://tomnabbe.com

http://www.wdwinfo.com/best-kept-secrets_Misc.htm

http://www.yesterland.com/ryman.html

FILM, TELEVISION, AND MUSEUM RESOURCES

Disneyland. TV Show. ABC. 1954-1958.

Disneyland Secrets, Stories and Magic. DVD. Walt Disney Video, 2007.

The Disney Family Museum, San Francisco, California.

Walt Disney Treasures: Disneyland USA. DVD. Walt Disney Video, 2001.

ADDITIONAL RECOMMENDED RESOURCES BOOKS

Allen, David. *Getting Things Done: The Art of Stress-Free Productivity*. New

York, NY: Penguin, 2001.

Amabile, Teresa and Steven Kramer. *The Progress Principle: Using Small Wins to Ignite Joy, Engagement, and Creativity at Work.* Boston, MA: Harvard Business Review Press, 2011.

Andrews, Andy. *The Noticer: Sometimes, All a Person Needs Is a Little Perspective.* Nashville, TN: Thomas Nelson Publishers, 2009.

Andrews, Andy. *The Traveler's Gift: Seven Decisions That Determine Personal Success.* Nashville, TN: Thomas Nelson Publishers, 2002.

Barrett, Steven M. *Disneyland's Hidden Mickeys: A Field Guide to Disneyland Resort's Best Kept Secrets.* Branford, CT: The Intrepid Traveler, 2013.

Bennett, Sam. *Get It Done: From Procrastination to Creative Genius in 15 Minutes a Day.* Novato, CA: New World Library, 2014.

Bright, Randy. *Disneyland: Inside Story.* New York, NY: Harry N. Abrams, Inc., 1987.

Catmull, Ed. *Creativity, Inc.: Overcoming the Unseen Forces That Stand in the Way of True Inspiration.* New York, NY: Random House, 2014.

Cockerell, Lee. *Creating Magic: 10 Common Sense Leadership Strategies from a Life at Disney.* New York, NY: Doubleday. 2008.

Covey, Stephen M. *The Speed of Trust: The One Thing That Changes Everything.* New York, NY: Free Press, 2006.

Crump, Rolly and Jeff Heimbuch. *It's Kind of a Cute Story.* Bamboo Forest Publishing, 2012.

Disney Institute. *Be Our Guest: Perfecting the Art of Customer Service.* New York, NY: Disney Editions, 2001.

Donovan, Jeremey. *How to Deliver a Ted Talk: Secrets of the World's Most Inspiring Presentations.* New York, NY: McGraw Hill Education, 2014.

Duhigg, Charles. *The Power of Habit: Why We Do What We Do in Life and Business.* New York, NY: Random House, 2012.

Dunlop, Beth. *Building A Dream: The Art of Disney Architecture.* New York, NY: Harry N. Abrams, Inc., 1996.

Emerson, Ralph Waldo. "Self-Reliance." *Self-Reliance and Other Essays.* New York, NY: Dover Books, 2012.

Fine, Alan. *You Already Know How to Be Great: A Simple Way to Remove Interference and Unlock Your Greatest Potential.* New York, NY: The Penguin Group, 2010.

Francaviglia, Richard V. *Main Street Revisited: Time, Space, and Image Building in Small-Town America.* Iowa City: University of Iowa Press, 1996.

Gabler, Neal. *Walt Disney: The Triumph of the American Imagination.* New York, NY: Random House, 2006.

Gallo, Carmine. *The Presentation Secrets of Steve Jobs: How to Be Insanely Great in Front of Any Audience.* New York, NY: McGraw Hill, 2010.

Gibson, Tyrese. *How to Get Out of Your Own Way.* New York, NY: Grand Central Publishing, 2011.

Gitomer, Jeffrey. *Customer Satisfaction Is Worthless, Customer Loyalty Is Priceless: How to Make Customers Love You, Keep Them Coming Back and Tell* Everyone *They Know.* Austin, TX: Bard Press, 1998.

Gladwell, Malcolm. *David and Goliath: Underdogs, Misfits, and the Art of Battling Giants.* New York, NY: Little Brown and Company, 2013.

Guillebeau, Chris. *The Art of Non-Conformity: Set Your Own Rules, Live the Life You Want, and Change the World.* New York, NY: Penguin Group. 2010.

Hansen, Katharine. *Tell Me About Yourself: Storytelling to Get Jobs and Propel Your Career.* Indianapolis, IN: JIST Works, 2009.

Harvey, Steve. *Act Like a Success, Think Like a Success: Discovering Your Gift and the Way to Life's Riches.* New York, NY: Amistad, 2014.

Hench, John. *Designing Disney: Imagineering and the Art of the Show.* New York, NY: Disney Editions, 2003.

Henry, Todd. *Die Empty: Unleash Your Best Work Every Day*. New York, NY: Penguin, 2013.

Imagineers, The. *Walt Disney Imagineering: A Behind the Dreams Look at Making the Magic Real*. New York, NY: Hyperion, 1996.

Jackson, Kathy Merlock and Mark West, eds. *Disneyland and Culture: Essays on the Parks and Their Influence*. Jefferson, NC: McFarland & Company, 2011.

Koenig, David. *Mouse Tales: A Behind-The-Ears Look at Disneyland*. Irvine, CA: Bonaventure Press, 1994.

Koenig, David. *More Mouse Tales: A Closer Peek Backstage at Disneyland*. Irvine, CA: Bonaventure Press, 1999.

Korkis, Jim. *The Vault of Walt*. Orlando, FL: Theme Park Press, 2010.

Korkis, Jim. *The Vault of Walt: Volume 3*. Orlando, FL: Theme Park Press, 2014.

Mumford, David and Bruce Gordon. *Disneyland the Nickel Tour: A Postcard Journey Through 40 Years of the Happiest Place on Earth*. Camphor Tree Publisher, 1995.

Pressfield, Steven. *Turning Pro. Tap Your Inner Power and Create Your Life's Work*. New York, NY: Black Irish Entertainment LLC., 2012.

Schultz, Jason and Kevin Yee. *Disneyland Almanac: Complete Park Information 1955-2010*. Zauberreich Press, 2011.

Simmons, Annette. *Whoever Tells the Best Story Wins: How to Use Your Own Stories to Communicate with Power and Impact*. New York, NY: AMACOM, 2007.

Sinek, Simon. *Leaders Eat Last: Why Some Teams Pull Together and Others Don't*. New York, NY: Penguin, 2014.

Snow, Patrick. *Creating Your Own Destiny: How to Get Exactly What You Want Out of Life and Work*. Hoboken, NJ: John Wiley & Sons, 2010.

Staver, Mike. *Do You Know How to Shut Up?* Fernandina Beach, FL: Mac

Daddy Publishing, 2008.

Strodder, Chris. *The Disneyland Book of Lists: Unofficial, Unauthorized, and Unprecedented*. Solano Beach, CA: Santa Monica Press, LLC., 2015.

Strodder, Chris. *The Disneyland Encyclopedia: The Unofficial, Unauthorized, and Unprecedented History of Every Land, Attraction, Restaurant, Shop, and Major Event in the Original Magic Kingdom*. Solano Beach, CA: Santa Monica Press, 2012.

Tracy, Brian. *Eat That Frog! 21 Great Ways to Stop Procrastinating and Get More Done in Less Time*. San Francisco, CA: Berrett-Koehler Publishers, Inc., 2007.

Wright, Alex. *The Imagineering Field Guide to Disneyland*. New York, NY: Disney Editions, 2008.

ONLINE RESOURCES

http://freshbakeddisney.com

http://www.jimhillmedia.com

http://www.laughingplace.com

http://www.mouseplanet.com

http://www.samlanddisney.blogspot.com

http://www.themeparkinsider.com

Made in the USA
Middletown, DE
13 November 2020

23826815R10141